William Winter

English Rambles

And other Fugitive Pieces in Prose and Verse

William Winter

English Rambles
And other Fugitive Pieces in Prose and Verse

ISBN/EAN: 9783337372330

Printed in Europe, USA, Canada, Australia, Japan

Cover: Foto ©Thomas Meinert / pixelio.de

More available books at **www.hansebooks.com**

ENGLISH RAMBLES:

AND

OTHER FUGITIVE PIECES,

In Prose and Verse.

BY

WILLIAM WINTER.

> "*I should love to go with you, — as I have gone, God knows how often, — into Little Britain, and Eastcheap, and Green Arbour Court, and Westminster Abbey. I should like to travel with you, outside of the last of the coaches, down to Bracebridge Hall.*" — CHARLES DICKENS.

BOSTON:
JAMES R. OSGOOD AND COMPANY.
1884.

✠

TO
LAWRENCE BARRETT,
IN WHOSE
THOUGHTFUL AND SYMPATHETIC
COMPANIONSHIP
THESE RAMBLES WERE ENJOYED,
AND BY WHOSE
FRIENDSHIP DURING MANY YEARS,
THE AUTHOR
HAS BEEN HONOURED AND CHEERED,
𝔗𝔥𝔦𝔰 𝔙𝔬𝔩𝔲𝔪𝔢
IS AFFECTIONATELY INSCRIBED.

✠

PREFACE.

✠

BEAUTIFUL and storied scenes which have soothed and elevated the mind naturally inspire a feeling of gratitude. It is this feeling which prompted the author of the present volume to write a record of his English Rambles. It also was his wish, in dwelling thus upon the rural loveliness and the literary and historical associations of England, to afford sympathetic guidance and useful suggestion to other American travellers, who, like himself, might be attracted to roam among the shrines of our mother land. There is no pursuit more fascinating, or, in a high intellectual sense, more remunerative; since it serves to define and regulate the stores of knowledge which have been acquired by reading, to correct misapprehensions of fact, to broaden the mental vision, to ripen and refine the judgment and the taste, and to fill the memory with ennobling recollections. These English Rambles are designed as a companion to the Trip to England. They were first published in the New York Tribune; they are now reprinted, in a revised form. In that journal also were first published the author's commemorative tributes to Longfellow, which are included in this book. The article on the Poet's Death was written in the evening of the day on which he died, and the Personal Recollections and the Elegy a few days afterwards. The Poems here presented have hitherto been Wanderers — as their collective title declares. Two of them, "In Sanctuary" and "W. A. S.," were first published in Harper's Magazine. Most of them are now for the first time brought together: and it is hoped that they may find favour, at least with those readers who have accepted with generous kindness the previous poetical writings of the same pen.

W. W.

Fort Hill, New Brighton, Staten Island,
    August 15, 1883.

CONTENTS.

✣

I.

ENGLISH RAMBLES.

I.	UP TO LONDON	11
II.	OLD CHURCHES OF LONDON	17
III.	LITERARY SHRINES OF LONDON	26
IV.	A HAUNT OF EDMUND KEAN	34
V.	STOKE POGIS AND THOMAS GRAY	40
VI.	AT THE GRAVE OF COLERIDGE	47
VII.	ON BARNET BATTLE-FIELD	55
VIII.	A GLIMPSE OF CANTERBURY	60
IX.	THE SHRINES OF WARWICKSHIRE	67
X.	A BORROWER OF THE NIGHT	81

II.

IN MEMORY OF LONGFELLOW.

I.	THE POET'S DEATH	93
II.	PERSONAL RECOLLECTIONS	99
III.	ELEGY	113

WANDERERS.

The Wrecker's Bell	119
Accomplices	126
A Dream of the Past	128
Homeward Bound	134
A Poet's Life	141
The Merry Monarch	146
Blue Eyes and Black	149
Old Times	151
John McCullough	153
Lawrence Barrett	158
In Honour of William Warren	162
W. A. S.	167
White Roses	171
In Sanctuary	173

ENGLISH RAMBLES.
1882.

✠

*"All that I saw returns upon my view;
  All that I heard comes back upon my ear;
  All that I felt this moment doth renew."*

———

*"Fair land! by Time's parental love made free,
  By Social Order's watchful arms embraced,
  With unexampled union meet in thee,
  For eye and mind, the present and the past;
  With golden prospect for futurity,
  If that be reverenced which ought to last."*
                                                WORDSWORTH.

✠.

ENGLISH RAMBLES.

I.

UP TO LONDON.

ABOUT the middle of the night the great ship comes to a pause, off the coast of Ireland, and, looking forth across the black waves, and through the rifts in the rising mist, we see the low and lonesome verge of that land of trouble and misery. A beautiful white light flashes now and then from the shore, and at intervals the mournful booming of a solemn bell floats over the sea. Soon is heard the rolling click of oars, and then two or three dusky boats glide past the ship, and hoarse voices hail and answer. A few stars are visible in the hazy sky, and the breeze from the land brings off, in fitful puffs, the fragrant balm of grass and clover, mingled with the salty odors of sea-weed and slimy rocks. There is a sense of mystery over the whole wild scene; but we realize now that human companionship is near, and that the long and lonely ocean voyage is ended.

Travellers who make the run from Liverpool to London by the Midland Railway pass through the Vale of Derby, and skirt around the stately Peak that Scott has commemorated in his novel of "Peveril." It is a more rugged country than is seen in the transit by the Northwestern road, but not more beautiful. You see the storied mountain, in all its delicacy of outline and all its airy magnificence of poise, soaring into the sky — its summit almost lost in the smoky haze — and you wind through hillside pastures and meadow lands that are curiously intersected with low, zigzag stone walls; and constantly, as the scene changes, you catch glimpses of green lane and shining river; of dense copses that cast their cool shadow on the moist and gleaming emerald sod; of long white roads that stretch away like cathedral aisles, and are lost beneath the leafy arches of elm and oak; of little church turrets embowered in ivy; of thatch cottages draped with roses; of dark ravines, luxuriant with a wild profusion of rocks and trees; and of golden grain that softly waves and whispers in the summer wind; while, all around, the grassy banks and glimmering meadows are radiant with yellow daisies, and with that wonderful scarlet of the poppy which gives an almost human glow of life and loveliness to the whole face of England. After some hours of such a pageant — so novel, so fascinating, so fleeting, so stimulative of eager curiosity and poetic desire — it is a relief at last to stand in the populous streets and among the grim houses of London, with its surging tides of life, and its turmoil of effort, conflict, exultation, and misery. How strange it seems — yet, at the same time, how homelike and familiar! There soars aloft the great dome of St. Paul's Cathedral, with its golden cross that flashes in the sunset! There stands the Victoria Tower — fit emblem of the true royalty of the sovereign whose name it bears. And there, more lowly but more august, rise the sacred turrets of the Abbey. It is the same old London — the great heart of the modern world — the great city of our reverence and love. As the wanderer writes these words he hears the plashing of the fountains in Trafalgar Square and the evening chimes that peal out from the spire of St. Martin's-in-the-Fields, and he knows himself once more at the shrine of all his youthful dreams.

To the observant stranger in London few sights can be more impressive than those which illustrate the singular manner in which the life of the present encroaches upon the memorials of the past. Old Temple Bar has gone, and only a column, at the junction of Fleet Street and the Strand, denotes where once it stood. The Midland Railway trains dash over what was once St. Pancras Churchyard — the burial-place of Mary Wollstonecraft, and of many other British worthies — and passengers looking from the carriages may see the children of the neighbourhood sporting among the few tombs that yet remain in that despoiled cemetery. Dolly's Chop House, intimately associated with the wits of the reign of Queen Anne, has been destroyed. The ancient tavern of "The Cock," immortalized by Tennyson, in his poem of "Will Waterproof's Monologue," is soon to disappear, — with its singular wooden entry, that existed before the time of the Plague, and that escaped the Great Fire of 1666. On the site of Northumberland House stands the Grand Hotel. The gravestones that formerly paved the yard of Westminster Abbey have been removed, to make way for grassy lawns intersected with pathways. In Southwark, across the Thames, the engine-room of the brewery of Messrs. Barclay & Perkins occupies the site of the Globe Theatre, that Shakespeare managed. One of the most venerable and beautiful churches in London, that of St. Bartholomew the Great, — a gray, mouldering temple, of the twelfth century, hidden away in a corner of Smithfield, and now become so poor that it has to beg sixpence from every visitor, — is desecrated by the irruption of an adjacent shop, the staircase hall of which breaks cruelly into the sacred edifice and impends above the altar. As lately as the 12th of July, 1882, the present writer, walking in the churchyard of St. Paul's, Covent Garden, — the sepulchre of William Wycherley, Robert Wilks, Charles Macklin, Joseph Haines, Thomas King, Samuel Butler, Thomas Southerne, Edward Shuter, Dr. Arne, Thomas Davies, Edward Kynaston, Richard Estcourt, William Havard, and many other renowned votaries of literature and the stage, — found workmen building a new wall to sustain the enclosure, and almost every stone in the cemetery uprooted and leaning against the adjacent houses. These monuments, it was said, would be replaced; but it was impossible not to consider the chances of error, in a new mortuary deal — and the grim witticism of Rufus Choate, about dilating with the wrong emotion, came then into remembrance, and did not come amiss.

Facts such as these, however, bid us remember how even the relics of the past are passing away, and that cities, unlike human creatures, may grow to be so old that at last they will become new. It is not wonderful, that London should change its aspect from one decade to another, as the living surmount and obliterate the dead. Thomas Sutton's Charter House School, founded in 1611, when Shakespeare and Ben Jonson were still writing, was reared upon ground in which several thousand corpses were buried, during the time of the Indian Pestilence of 1348; and it still stands and flourishes. Nine thousand new houses, it is said, are built in the great capital every year, and twenty-eight miles of new streets are thus added to it. On a Sunday I drove for three hours through the eastern part of London, without coming upon a single trace of the open fields. On the west, all the region from Kensington to Richmond is settled for most part of the way; while northward the city is stretching its arms toward Hampstead, Highgate, and tranquil and blooming Finchley. Truly the spirit of this age is in strong contrast with that of the time of Henry the Eighth when (1580), to prevent the increasing size of London, all new buildings were forbidden to be erected "where no former hath been known to have been." The march of improvement nowadays carries everything before it: even British conservatism is at some points giving way: and, noting the changes which have occurred here within only five years, I am persuaded that those who would see what remains of the London of which they have read and dreamed — the London of Dryden and Pope, of Addison, Sheridan and Byron, of Betterton, Garrick, and Edmund Kean — will, as time passes, find more and more difficulty both in tracing the footsteps of fame, and in finding that sympathetic, reverent spirit which hallows the relics of genius and renown.

II.

OLD CHURCHES OF LONDON.

SIGHT-SEEING, merely for its own sake, is not to be commended. Hundreds of persons roam through the storied places of England, carrying nothing away but the bare sense of travel. It is not the spectacle that benefits, but the meaning of the spectacle. In the great temples of religion, in those wonderful cathedrals which are the glory of the old world, we ought to feel, not merely the physical beauty, but the perfect, illimitable faith, the passionate, incessant devotion, which alone made them possible. The cold intellect of a sceptical age — like the present — could never create such a majestic cathedral as that of Canterbury. Not till the pilgrim feels this truth has he really learned the lesson of such places, — to keep alive in his heart the capacity of self-sacrifice, of toil and of tears, for the grandeur and beauty of the spiritual life. At the tombs of great men we ought to feel something more than a consciousness of the crumbling clay that moulders within, — something more even than knowledge of their memorable words and deeds: we ought, as we ponder on the certainty of death and the evanescence of earthly things, to realize that Art at least is permanent, and that no creature can be better employed than in noble effort to make the soul worthy of immortality. The relics of the past, contemplated merely because they are relics, are nothing. You tire, in this old land, of the endless array of ruined castles and of wasting graves; you sicken at the thought of the mortality of a thousand years, decaying at your feet, and you long to look again on roses and the face of childhood, the ocean and the stars. But not if the meaning of the past is truly within your sympathy; not if you perceive its associations as feeling equally with knowledge; not if you truly know that its lessons are not of death but of life! To-day builds over the ruins of yesterday, as well in the soul of man as on the vanishing cities that mark his course. There need be no regret that, in this sense, the present should obliterate the past.

Much, however, as London has changed, and constantly as it continues to change, there still remain, and long will continue to remain, many objects that startle and impress the sensitive mind. Through all its wide compass, by night and day, there flows and beats a turbulent, resounding tide of activity, and hundreds of trivial and vacuous people, sordid, ignorant, and commonplace, tramp to and fro amid its storied antiquities, heedless of their existence. Through such surroundings, but finding here and there a sympathetic guide or a friendly suggestion, the explorer must take his way, — lonely in the crowd, and walking, indeed, like one who lives in a dream. Yet he never will drift in vain through a city like this. I went, one night, into the cloisters of Westminster Abbey — that part, the South Walk, which is still accessible after the gates have been closed. The stars shone down upon the blackening walls and glimmering windows of the great cathedral; the grim, mysterious arches were dimly lighted; the stony pathways, stretching away beneath the venerable building, seemed to lose themselves in caverns of darkness ; not a sound was heard but the faint rustling of the grass within the close. Every stone here is the mark of a sepulchre ; every breath of the night-wind seemed the whisper of a gliding ghost. Here, among the crowded graves, rest Anne Oldfield and Anne Bracegirdle, — in Queen Anne's reign, such brilliant luminaries of the stage, — and here was buried the dust of Aaron Hill, poet and dramatist, the old manager of Drury Lane, who wrote "The Fair Inconstant" for Barton Booth, and some notably sweet and felicitous love-songs. Here, too, are the relics of Susanna Maria Anne (Mrs. Theo. Cibber), Aphra Behn, Thomas Betterton, and Spranger Barry. Sitting upon the narrow ledge which was the monks' rest, I could touch, close at hand, the tomb of a mitred Abbot, while at my feet was the great stone that covers twenty-six monks of Westminster who perished by the Plague nearly six hundred years ago. It would scarcely be believed that the doors of dwellings open upon this gloomy spot; that women may sometimes be seen tending flowers upon the ledges that roof these cloister walks. Yet so it is; and in such a place, at such a time, you comprehend, better than before, the self-centred, serious, ruminant, romantic character of the English mind, — which loves, more than anything else in the world, the privacy of august surroundings and a sombre and stately solitude. It need hardly be said that you likewise obtain here a striking sense of the power of contrast. I was again aware of this, a little later, when, seeing a dim light in St. Margaret's Church near by, I entered that old temple, and found the boys of the choir at their rehearsal, and presently observed on the wall a brass plate which announces that Sir Walter Raleigh was buried here, in the chancel, after being decapitated for high treason in the Palace Yard outside. Such things are the surprises of this historic capital, — the exceeding great reward of the wanderer's devotion. This inscription begs the reader to remember Raleigh's virtues as well as his faults, — a plea, surely, that every man might well wish should be made for himself at last. I thought of the verses that the old warrior-poet is said to have left in his Bible, when they led him out to die :

> "Even such is time ; that takes in trust
>   Our youth, our joys, our all we have,
> And pays us nought but age and dust ;
>   Which, in the dark and silent grave,
> When we have wandered all our ways,
>   Shuts up the story of our days. —
> But from this earth, this grave, this dust,
>   My God shall raise me up, I trust."

In St. Margaret's [1] — a storied haunt, for shining names alike of nobles and poets — was also buried John Skelton, another of the old bards (obiit 1529), the enemy and satirist of Cardinal Wolsey and Sir

---

[1] This church contains a window, commemorative of Raleigh, presented by Americans, and inscribed with these lines, by Lowell :

> The New World's sons, from England's breast we drew
>   Such milk as bids remember whence we came :
> Proud of her past, wherefrom our future grew,
>   This window we inscribe with Raleigh's name.

It also contains a window, commemorative of Caxton, presented by the printers and publishers of London, which is inscribed with these lines, by Tennyson :

> Thy prayer was Light — more Light — while Time shall last.
>   Thou sawest a glory growing on the night,
> But not the shadows which that light would cast
>   Till shadows vanish in the Light of Light.

Thomas More, one of whom he described as "madde Amaleke," and the other as "dawcock doctor." Their renown has managed to survive these terrific shafts; but at least this was a falcon who flew at eagles. Here the poet Campbell was married, — October 11th, 1803. Such old churches as this — guarding so well their treasures of history — are, in a special sense, the traveller's blessings. At St. Giles's, Cripplegate, the janitor is a woman; and she will point out to you the lettered stone that formerly marked the grave of Milton. It is in the nave, but it has been moved to a place about twelve feet from its original position, — the remains of the illustrious poet being, in fact, beneath the floor of a pew, on the left of the central aisle, about the middle of the church: albeit there is a story, possibly true, that, on an occasion when this church was repaired, in August, 1790, the coffin of Milton suffered profanation, and his bones were dispersed. Among the monuments hard by is a fine marble bust of Milton, placed against the wall, and it is said, by way of enhancing its value, that George the Third came here to see it. Several of the neighbouring inscriptions are of astonishing quaintness. They claim the dust of Daniel De Foe for this church, but cannot designate his grave. The adjacent churchyard — a queer, irregular, sequestered, lonesome bit of grassy ground, teeming with monuments, and hemmed in with houses, terminates, at one end, in a piece of the old Roman wall of London (A. D. 306), — an adamantine structure of cemented flints — which has lasted from the days of Julius Cæsar, and which bids fair to last forever. I shall always remember this strange nook with the golden light of a summer morning shining upon it, the birds twittering among its graves, and all around it such an atmosphere of solitude and rest as made it seem, though in the heart of the great city, a thousand miles from any haunt of man.

At St. Helen's, Bishopgate, also, the janitor is a woman, and one who knows and loves every monument in this ancient and venerable temple — the church of the priory of the nuns of St. Helen, built in the thirteenth century, and full of relics of the history of England. The priory, which adjoined this church, has long since disappeared, and portions of the building have been restored; but the noble Gothic columns and the commemorative sculpture remain unchanged. Here are the tombs of Sir John Crosby, who built Crosby Place (1466), Sir Thomas Gresham, who founded both Gresham College and the Royal Exchange in London, and Sir William Pickering, once Queen Elizabeth's Minister to Spain and one of the amorous aspirants for her royal hand; and here, in a gloomy chapel, stands the veritable altar at which the cruel and crafty Duke of Gloster received absolution, after he had despatched the princes to the Tower. Standing at that altar, in the cool silence of the lonely church and the waning light of afternoon, it was easy to conjure up his slender, misshapen form, decked out in the rich apparel that he loved, his handsome, aquiline, thoughtful face, the drooping head, the glittering, baleful eyes, the nervous hand that toyed with the dagger, and the stealthy stillness of his person, from head to foot, as he knelt there before the priest and mocked himself and heaven with the form of prayer. Every place that Richard touched is haunted by his magnetic presence: no place more strangely so than this! In another part of the church you are shown the tomb of a knight whose will provided that the key of his sepulchre should be placed beside his body, and that the door should be opened once a year, for a hundred years. It seems to have been his expectation to awake and arise; but the allotted century has passed and his knightly bones are still quiescent.

How calmly they sleep — these warriors who once filled the world with the tumult of their deeds! If you go into Saint Mary's, in the Temple, — one of the noblest Gothic buildings in England, — you will stand above the dust of the Crusaders, and mark the beautiful copper effigies of them, recumbent on the marble pavement, and feel and know, as perhaps you never did before, the calm that follows the tempest. Saint Mary's was built in 1240, and restored in 1828. It would be difficult to find a lovelier specimen of Norman Gothic architecture — at once massive and airy, perfectly simple, yet rich with beauty, in every line and scroll. There is only one other church in Great Britain, it is said, which has, like this, a circular vestibule. The stained glass windows, both here and at St. Helen's, are very glorious. The organ at St. Mary's was selected by Jeffries, afterwards infamous as the wicked judge. The pilgrim who pauses to muse at the grave of Goldsmith may often hear its solemn, mournful tones. I heard them thus, and was thinking of Doctor Johnson's tender words, when he first learned that Goldsmith was dead: "Poor Goldy was wild — very wild — but he is so no more." The room in which he died, a brokenhearted man at only forty-six, was but a little way from the spot where he sleeps.[1] The noises of Fleet Street are heard there only as a distant murmur. But birds chirp over him, and leaves flutter down upon his tomb, and every breeze that sighs around the gray turrets of the ancient Temple breathes out his requiem.

[1] No. 2 Brick Court, Middle Temple. — In 1757–58 Goldsmith was employed by a chemist, near Fish Street Hill. When he wrote his "Inquiry into the Present State of Polite Learning in Europe" he was living in Green Arbour Court, "over Break-neck Steps." At a lodging in Wine Office Court, Fleet Street, he wrote "The Vicar of Wakefield." Afterwards he had lodgings at Canonbury House, Islington, and in 1764, in the Library Staircase of the Inner Temple.

III.

LITERARY SHRINES OF LONDON.

THE mind that can reverence historic associations needs no explanation of the charm that such associations possess. There are streets and houses in London which, for pilgrims of this class, are haunted with memories and hallowed with an imperishable light—that not even the dreary commonness of every-day life can quench or dim. Almost every great author in English literature has here left behind him some personal trace, some relic that brings us at once into his living presence. In the days of Shakespeare,—of whom it may be noted that wherever you find him at all you find him in select and elegant neighbourhoods,—Bishopgate was a retired and aristocratic quarter of the town;

and here the poet had his residence, convenient to
the theatre in Blackfriars, of which he was an
owner. It is said that he dwelt very near to Crosby
Place, and certainly he saw that building in its
splendour, and, no doubt, was often in St. Helen's
Church, near by; and upon this spot, — amid all
the din of traffic and all the strange adjuncts of a
new age, — those who love him are in his company.
Milton was born in a court adjacent to Bread Street,
Cheapside, and the explorer comes upon him as a
resident in St. Bride's Churchyard, — where the
poet Lovelace was buried, — and at the house which
is now No. 19 York Street, Queen's Square (in later
times occupied by Bentham and by Hazlitt), and
in Jewin Street, Aldersgate. When Secretary to
Cromwell he lived in Scotland Yard, where now is
the headquarters of the London police. His last
home was in Artillery Walk, Bunhill Fields, but the
visitor to that ground finds it covered by the Artillery
Barracks. Walking through King Street, Westminster, you will not forget Edmund Spenser, who died
there, in grief and destitution, a victim to the same
inhuman spirit of Irish ruffianism which is still disgracing humanity and troubling the peace of the
world. Everybody remembers Ben Jonson's terse
record of this calamity: "The Irish having robbed
Spenser's goods and burnt his house and a little
child new-born, he and his wife escaped, and after
he died, for lack of bread, in King Street." Jonson
himself is closely and charmingly associated with

places that may still be seen. He passed his boyhood near Charing Cross — having been born in Hartshorne Lane, now Northumberland Street — and went to the parish school of St. Martin's-in-the-Fields; and those who roam around Lincoln's Inn will surely call to mind that this great poet helped to build it — a trowel in one hand and Horace in the other. His residence, in his days of fame, was just outside of Temple Bar — but all that neighbourhood is new at the present day.

The Mermaid, which he frequented — with Shakespeare, Fletcher, Herrick, Chapman, and Donne — was in Bread Street, but no trace of it remains; and a banking house (Child's Bank) stands now on the site of the Devil Tavern, in Fleet Street, where the Apollo Club, which he founded, used to meet. The famous inscription, "O rare Ben Jonson," is three times cut in the Abbey — once in Poets' Corner, and twice in the north aisle where he was buried, the smaller of the two slabs marking the place of his vertical grave. Dryden once dwelt in a narrow, dingy, quaint little house, in Fetter Lane, — the street in which Dean Swift has placed the home of Gulliver, and where now the famous Doomsday Book is kept, — but later he removed to a finer dwelling, in Gerrard Street, Soho, which was the scene of his death. Both buildings are marked with mural tablets, and neither of them seems to have undergone much change. Edmund Burke's house, also in Gerrard Street, is let in lodgings and licensed to sell beer; but his memory hallows the place, and an inscription upon it proudly announces that here he lived. Dr. Johnson's house in Gough Square bears likewise a mural tablet, and, standing at its time-worn threshold, the visitor needs no effort of fancy to picture that uncouth figure shambling through the crooked lanes that lead into this queer, sombre, confined, and melancholy retreat. In this house he wrote the first Dictionary of the English language, and the immortal letter to Lord Chesterfield. In Gough Square lived and died Hugh Kelly, dramatist, author of "The School of Wives" and "The Man of Reason," and one of the friends of Goldsmith, at whose burial he was present. The historical antiquarian society that has marked these literary shrines of London has, surely, rendered a great service. The houses associated with Reynolds and Hogarth, in Leicester Square, Byron, in Holles Street, Benjamin Franklin and Peter the Great, in Craven Street, Campbell, in Duke Street, St. James's, Garrick, in the Adelphi Terrace, and Mrs. Siddons, in Baker Street, are but a few of the historic spots which are thus commemorated. Much, however, yet remains to be done. One would like to know, for instance, in which room in "The Albany" it was that Byron wrote "Lara,"[1] in which of the houses in Buckingham

---

[1] Byron was born at No. 24 Holles Street, Cavendish Square. While he was at school in Dulwich Grove his mother lived in a house in Sloane Terrace. Other houses associated with him are

Street Coleridge had his lodging, while he was translating "Wallenstein"; whereabouts in Bloomsbury Square was the residence of Akenside, who wrote "The Pleasures of Imagination," and of Croly, who wrote "Salathiel"; or where it was that Gray lived, when he established himself close by Russell Square, in order to be one of the first, — as he continued to be one of the most constant, — students at the then newly opened British Museum (1759). These, and such as these, may seem trivial things; but Nature has denied an unfailing source of innocent happiness to the man who can find no pleasure in them. For my part, when rambling in Fleet Street, it is a special delight to remember even so slight an incident as that recorded of the author of the "Elegy in a Country Churchyard," — that he once saw here his satirist, Dr. Johnson, rolling and puffing along the sidewalk, and cried out to a friend, "Here comes Ursa Major." For the true lovers of literature "Ursa Major" walks oftener in Fleet Street to-day than any living man.

A good thread of literary research might be profit-

No. 8 St. James Street; a lodging in Bennet Street; No. 2 "The Albany" — a lodging that he rented of Lord Althorpe, and moved into on March 28th, 1814; and No. 13 Piccadilly Terrace, where his daughter, Ada, was born, and where Lady Byron left him. John Murray's house, where his fragment of Autobiography was burned, was in Albemarle Street. Byron's body, when brought home from Greece, lay in state at No. 25 Great George Street, Westminster, before being taken north, to Hucknall-Torkard Church, in Nottinghamshire, for burial.

ably followed by him who should trace the footsteps of all the poets that have held, in England, the office of laureate. John Kay was laureate in the reign of Edward IV.; Andrew Bernard in that of Henry VII.; John Skelton in that of Henry VIII.; and Edmund Spenser in that of Elizabeth. Since then the succession has included the names of Samuel Daniel, Michael Drayton, Ben Jonson, Sir William Davenant, John Dryden, Thomas Shadwell, Nahum Tate, Nicholas Rowe, Lawrence Eusden, Colley Cibber, William Whitehead, Thomas Warton, Henry James Pye, Robert Southey, William Wordsworth, and Alfred Tennyson — the latter still wearing, in spotless renown, that

> "Laurel greener from the brows
> Of him that uttered nothing base."

Most of these bards were intimately associated with London, and several of them are buried in the Abbey. It is, indeed, because so many storied names are written upon gravestones that the explorer of the old churches of London finds so rich a harvest of impressive association and lofty thought. Few persons visit them, and you are likely to find yourself comparatively alone in rambles of this kind. I went one morning into St. Martin's — once "in the fields," now in one of the busiest thoroughfares at the centre of the city — and found there only a pew-opener preparing for the service, and an organist playing an anthem. It is a beautiful structure, with its graceful spire and its columns of weather-beaten stone, curiously stained in gray and sooty black, and it is almost as famous for theatrical names as St. Paul's, Covent Garden, or St. George's, Bloomsbury, or St. Clement-le-Danes. Here, in a vault beneath the church, was buried the bewitching and large-hearted Nell Gwyn; here is the grave of James Smith, joint author with his brother Horace, — who was buried at Tunbridge Wells, — of "The Rejected Addresses"; here rests Yates, the original *Sir Oliver Surface;* and here were laid the ashes of the romantic and brilliant Mrs. Centlivre, and of George Farquhar, whom neither youth, genius, patient labour, nor splendid achievement could save from a life of misfortune and an untimely and piteous death. A cheerier association of this church is with Thomas Moore, the great poet of Ireland, who was here married. At St. Giles's-in-the-Fields, again, are the graves of George Chapman, who translated Homer, Andrew Marvel, who wrote such lovely lyrics of love, Rich, the manager, who brought out Gay's "Beggar's Opera," and James Shirley, the fine old dramatist and poet, whose immortal couplet has been so often murmured in such solemn haunts as these:

> "Only the actions of the just
> Smell sweet and blossom in the dust."

Shirley lived in Gray's Inn when he was writing his plays, and he was fortunate in the favour of Queen Henrietta Maria, wife to Charles the First; but, when the Puritan times came in, he fell into misfortune and poverty and became a school-teacher in Whitefriars. In 1666 he was living in or near Fleet Street, and his home was one of the many dwellings that were destroyed in the Great Fire. Then he fled, with his wife, into the parish of St. Giles's-in-the-Fields, where, overcome with grief and terror, they both died, within twenty-four hours of each other, and they were buried in the same grave.

IV.

A HAUNT OF EDMUND KEAN.

TO muse over the graves of those about whom we have read so much — the great actors, thinkers, and writers, the warriors and statesmen for whom the play is ended and the lights are put out — is to come very near to them, and to realize more deeply than ever before their close relationship with our own humanity; and we ought to be wiser and better for this experience. It is good, also, to seek out the favourite haunts of our heroes, and call them up as they were in their lives. One of the happiest accidents of a London stroll was the finding of the Harp Tavern,[1] in Russell Street, Covent

---

[1] An account of the "Harp," which I have lately found, in the "Victuallers' Gazette," says that this tavern has had within

Garden, near the stage door of Drury Lane Theatre, which was the accustomed resort of Edmund Kean. Carpenters and masons were at work upon it when I entered, and it was necessary almost to creep amid heaps of broken mortar and rubbish beneath their scaffolds, in order to reach the interior rooms. Here, at the end of a narrow passage, was a little apartment, perhaps fifteen feet square, with a low ceiling and a bare floor, in which Kean habitually took his pleasure, in the society of fellow actors and boon companions, long ago. A narrow, cushioned bench against the walls, a few small tables, a chair or two, a number of church-warden pipes on the mantelpiece, and portraits of Disraeli and Gladstone, constituted the furniture. A panelled wainscot and dingy red paper covered the walls, and a few cobwebs hung from the grimy ceiling. By this time the old room has been cleaned, re-papered and made spruce and tidy; but then it bore all the marks of hard usage and long neglect, and it seemed all the more interesting for that reason.

Kean's seat is at the right, as you enter, and just above it a mural tablet designates the spot, — which

its doors every actor of note since the days of Garrick, and many actresses, also, of the period of eighty or a hundred years ago; and it mentions as visitants here Dora Jordan, Nance Oldfield, Anne Bracegirdle, Kitty Clive, Harriet Mellon, Barton Booth, Quin, Cibber, Macklin, Grimaldi, Mme. Vestris, and Miss Stephens, — who became the Countess of Essex.

is still further commemorated by a death-mask of the actor, placed on a little shelf of dark wood and covered with glass. No better portrait could be desired; certainly no better one exists. In life this must have been a glorious face. The eyes are large and prominent, the brow is broad and fine, the mouth wide and obviously sensitive, the chin delicate, and the nose long, well-set, and indicative of immense force of character. The whole expression of the face is that of refinement and of great and desolate sadness. Kean, as is known from the testimony of one who acted with him,[1] was always at his best in passages of pathos. To hear him speak *Othello's* Farewell was to hear the perfect music of heart-broken despair. To see him when, as *The Stranger*, he listened to the song, was to see, through tears, the genuine, absolute reality of hopeless sorrow. He could, of course, thrill mankind in the ferocious outbursts of *Richard* and *Sir Giles*, but it was in tenderness and grief that he was supremely great; and no one will wonder at this, who looks upon his noble face — so eloquent

[1] The mother of Jefferson, the comedian, described Edmund Kean in this way. She was a member of the company at the Walnut Street Theatre, Philadelphia, when he acted there, and it was she who sang for him the well-known lines:

> "I have a silent sorrow here,
>   A grief I 'll ne'er impart;
> It breathes no sigh, it sheds no tear,
>   But it consumes my heart."

of self-conflict and suffering — even in this cold and colourless mask of death. It is easy to judge and condemn the sins of a weak, passionate humanity; but when we think of such creatures of genius as Edmund Kean and Robert Burns we ought to consider what demons in their own souls those wretched men were forced to fight, and by what agonies they expiated their vices and errors. This little tavern-room tells the whole mournful story, with death to point the moral, and pity to breathe its sigh of unavailing regret.

Many of the present frequenters of the Harp are elderly men, whose conversation is enriched with memories of the stage and with ample knowledge and judicious taste in literature and art. They naturally speak with pride of Kean's association with their favourite resort. Often in that room the eccentric genius has put himself in pawn, to exact from the manager of Drury Lane Theatre the money needed to relieve the wants of some brother actor. Often his voice has been heard there, in the songs that he sang with so much feeling and sweetness and such homely yet beautiful skill. In the circles of the learned and courtly he never was really at home; but here he filled the throne and ruled the kingdom of the revel, and here no doubt every mood of his mind, from high thought and generous emotion to misanthropical bitterness and vacant levity, found its unfettered expression. They show you a broken panel in the high wainscot, which was struck and smashed by a pewter pot, that he hurled at the head of a person who had given him offence; and they tell you, at the same time, — as, indeed, is historically true, — that he was the idol of his comrades, the first in love, pity, sympathy, and kindness, and would turn his back, any day, for the least of them, on the nobles who sought his companionship. There is no better place than this in which to study the life of Edmund Kean. Old men may be met with here, who saw him on the stage, and even acted with him. The room is the weekly meeting-place and habitual nightly tryst of an ancient club, called the City of Lushington, which has existed since the days of the Regency, and of which these persons are members. The City has its Mayor, Sheriff, insignia, record-book, and system of ceremonials; and much of wit, wisdom, and song may be enjoyed at its civic feasts. The names of its four wards — Lunacy, Suicide, Poverty, and Juniper — are written up in the four corners of the room, and whoever joins must select his ward. Sheridan was a member of it, and so was the Regent; and the present landlord of the Harp [Mr. McPherson] preserves among his relics the chairs in which these gay companions sat, when the author presided over the initiation of the prince. It is thought that this club originated, in fact, out of the society of "The Wolves," which was formed by Kean's adherents, when the elder Booth arose to disturb his supremacy upon the stage. But there is no malignity in it now. Its purposes are simply convivial and literary, and its tone is that of thorough good-will.

One of the gentlest and most winning traits in the English character is its instinct of companionship as to literature and art. Since the days of the Mermaid, the authors and actors of London have dearly loved and deeply enjoyed such odd little fraternities of wit as are typified, not inaptly, by the City of Lushington. There are no rosier hours in my memory than those that were passed, between midnight and morning, in the cosey rooms of the Beefsteak Club, in London. And, when dark days come, and foes harass, and the troubles of life annoy, it will be sweet to think that, in still another sacred retreat of friendship, across the sea, the old armour is gleaming in the festal lights, where one of the gentlest spirits that ever wore the laurel of England's love smiles kindly on his comrades and seems to murmur the mystical spell of English hospitality:

> "Let no one take beyond this threshold hence,
> Words uttered here in friendship's confidence."

V.

STOKE POGIS AND THOMAS GRAY.

IT is a cool afternoon in July, and the shadows are falling eastward on fields of waving grain and lawns of emerald velvet. Overhead a few light clouds are drifting, and the green boughs of the great elms are gently stirred by a breeze from the west. Across one of the more distant fields a flock of sable rooks — some of them fluttering and cawing — wings its slow and melancholy flight. There is the sound of the whetting of a scythe, and, near by, the twittering of many birds upon a cottage roof. On either side of the country road, which runs like a white rivulet through banks of green, the hawthorn hedges are shining, and the bright sod is spangled with all the wild flowers of an English summer. An odour of lime-trees and of new-mown hay sweetens the air, for miles and miles around. Far off, on the horizon's verge, just glimmering through the haze, rises the imperial citadel of Windsor. And close at hand a little child points to a gray spire peering out of a nest of ivy, and tells me that this is Stoke Pogis Church.

If peace dwells anywhere upon this earth, its dwelling-place is here. You come into this little churchyard by a pathway across the park, and through a wooden turnstile; and in one moment the whole world is left behind and forgotten. Here are the nodding elms; here is the yew-tree's shade; here "heaves the turf in many a mouldering heap." All these graves seem very old. The long grass waves over them, and some of the low stones that mark them are entirely shrouded with ivy. Many of the "frail memorials" are made of wood. None of them is neglected or forlorn, but all of them seem to have been scattered here, in that sweet disorder which is the perfection of rural loveliness. There never, of course, could have been any thought of creating this effect; yet here it remains, to win your heart forever. And here, amid this mournful beauty, the little church itself nestles close to the ground, while every tree that waves its branches around it, and every vine that clambers on its surface, seems to clasp it in the arms of love. Nothing breaks the silence but the sighing of the wind in the great yew-tree, at the church door,—beneath which was the poet's favourite seat, and where the brown needles, falling, through many an autumn, have made a dense carpet on the turf. Now and then there is a faint rustle in the ivy; a fitful bird-note serves but to deepen the stillness; and from a rose-tree near at hand a few leaves flutter down, in soundless benediction on the dust beneath.

Gray was laid in the same grave with his mother, "the careful, tender mother of many children, one alone of whom," as he wrote upon her gravestone, "had the misfortune to survive her." Their tomb — a low, oblong, brick structure, covered with a large slab — stands a few feet away from the church wall, upon which is a small tablet to denote its place. The poet's name has not been inscribed above him. There was no need here of "storied urn or animated bust." The place is his monument, and the majestic Elegy — giving to the soul of the place a form of seraphic beauty and a voice of celestial music — is his immortal epitaph:

> "Here scattered oft, the earliest of the year,
> By hands unseen are showers of violets found;
> The red-breast loves to build and warble here,
> And little footsteps lightly print the ground."

There is a monument to Gray in Stoke Park, about two hundred yards from the church; but it seems commemorative of the builder rather than the poet. They intend to set a memorial window in the church, to honour him, and the visitor finds there a money-box for the reception of contributions in aid of this pious design. Nothing will be done amiss that serves to direct closer attention to his life. It was one of the best lives ever recorded in the history of literature. It was a life singularly pure, noble, and beautiful. In two qualities, sincerity and reticence, it was exemplary almost beyond a parallel; and those are qualities which literary character in the present day has great need to acquire. Gray was averse to publicity. He did not sway by the censure of other men; neither did he need their admiration as his breath of life. Poetry, to him, was a great art; and he added nothing to literature until he had first made it as nearly perfect as it could be made by the thoughtful, laborious exertion of his best powers, superadded to the spontaneous impulse and flow of his genius. More voluminous writers, Charles Dickens among the rest, have sneered at him because he wrote so little. The most colossal form of human conceit, probably, is that of the individual who thinks all other creatures inferior who happen to be unlike himself. This reticence on the part of Gray was, in fact, the grand emblem of his sincerity and the corner-stone of his imperishable renown. There is a better thing than the great man who is always speaking; and that is the great man who only speaks when he has a great word to say. Gray has left only a few poems; but, of his principal works, each is perfect in its kind, supreme and unapproachable. He did not test merit by reference to ill-informed and capricious public opinion, but he wrought according to the highest standards of art that learning and taste could furnish. His Letters form an English classic. There is no better prose in existence; there is not much that is so good. But the crowning glory of Gray's nature, the element that makes it so impressive, the charm that brings the pilgrim to Stoke Pogis Church to muse upon it, was the self-poised, sincere, and lovely exaltation of its contemplative spirit. He was a man whose conduct of life would, first of all, purify, extend, and adorn the temple of his own soul, out of which should afterward flow, in their own free way, those choral harmonies that soothe, guide, and exalt the human race. He lived before he wrote. The soul of the Elegy is the soul of the man. It was his thought — which he has somewhere expressed in better words than these — that human beings are only at their best while such feelings endure as are engendered when death has just taken from us the objects of our love. That was the point of view from which he habitually looked upon the world; and no man who has learned the lessons of experience can doubt that he was right.

Gray was twenty-six years old when he wrote the first draft of the Elegy. He began this poem, in 1742, at Stoke Pogis, and he finished and published it in 1750. No visitor to this churchyard can miss either its inspiration or its imagery. The poet has been dead more than a hundred years; but the scene of his rambles and reveries has suffered no material change. One of his yew-trees, indeed, much weakened with age, was some time since blown down in a storm, and its fragments have been carried away. A picturesque house contiguous to the churchyard, which in Queen Elizabeth's time was a palace and was visited by that sovereign, and which Gray knew as a manor, has now become a dairy. All the trees of the region have, of course, waxed and expanded, — not forgetting the neighbouring beeches of Birnam, among which he loved to wander, and where he might often have been found, sitting with his book, at some gnarled wreath of "old fantastic roots." But, in all its general characteristics, its rustic homeliness and peaceful beauty, this "glimmering landscape," immortalized in his verse, is the same on which his living eyes have looked. There was no need to seek for him in any special spot. The cottage in which he once lived might, no doubt, be discovered; but every nook and vista, every green lane and upland lawn and ivy-mantled tower of this delicious solitude is haunted with his presence.

The night is coming on and the picture will soon be dark; but never while memory lasts can it fade out of the heart. What a blessing would be ours, if only we could hold forever that exaltation of the spirit, that sweet, resigned serenity, that pure freedom from all the passions of nature and all the cares of life, which comes upon us in such a place as this! Alas, and again Alas! Even with the thought this golden mood begins to melt away; even with the thought comes our dismissal from its influence. Nor will it avail us anything now to linger at the shrine. Fortunate is he, though in bereavement and regret, who parts from beauty while yet her kiss is warm upon his lips, — waiting not for the last farewell word, hearing not the last notes of the music, seeing not the last gleams of sunset as the light dies from the sky. It was a sad parting, but the memory of the place can never now be despoiled of its loveliness. As I write these words I stand again in the cool and dusky silence of the poet's church, with its air of stately age and its fragrance of cleanliness, while the light of the western sun, broken into rays of gold and ruby, streams through the great painted windows, and softly falls upon the quaint little galleries and decorous pews; and, looking forth through the low, arched door, I see the dark and melancholy boughs of the dreaming yew-tree, and, nearer, a shadow of rippling leaves in the clear sunshine of the churchway path. And all the time a quiet voice is whispering, in the chambers of thought:

> "No farther seek his merits to disclose,
> Or draw his frailties from their dread abode,
> (There they alike in trembling hope repose),
> The bosom of his Father and his God."

VI.

AT THE GRAVE OF COLERIDGE.

AMONG the many deep-thoughted, melodious and eloquent poems of Wordsworth there is one — about the burial of Ossian — which glances at the question of fitness in a place of sepulture. Not always, for the illustrious dead, has the final couch of rest been rightly chosen. We think with resignation, and with a kind of pride, of Keats and Shelley in the little Protestant burial-ground at Rome. Every heart is touched at the spectacle of Garrick and Johnson sleeping side by side in Westminster Abbey. It was right that the dust of Dean Stanley should mingle with the dust of poets and of kings; and to see — as the present writer did, only a little while ago — fresh flowers on the stone that covers him, in the chapel of Henry the Seventh, was to feel a tender gladness and solemn content. Shakespeare's grave, in the chancel of Stratford Church, awakens the same ennobling awe and melancholy pleasure; and it is with kindred feelings that you linger at the tomb of Gray. But who can be content that poor Letitia Landon should sleep beneath the pavement of a barrack, with soldiers trampling over her dust? One might almost think, sometimes, that the spirit of calamity, which follows certain persons throughout the whole of life, had pursued them even in death, to haunt about their repose and to mar all the gentleness of association that ought to hallow it. Chatterton, a pauper and a suicide, was huddled into a workhouse graveyard, the very place of which — in Shoe Lane, covered now by Farringdon Market — has disappeared. Otway, miserable in his love for Elizabeth Barry, the actress, and said to have starved to death, in the Minories, near the Tower of London, was laid in a vault of St. Clement-le-Danes in the middle of the Strand, where never the green leaves rustle, but where the roar of the mighty city pours on in continual tumult. This church holds also the remains of William Mountfort, the actor, slain in a brawl by Lord Mohun; of Nat Lee, "the mad poet"; of George Powell, the tragedian, of brilliant and deplorable memory; and of the handsome Hildebrand Horden,[1] cut off by a

---

[1] Hildebrand Horden was the son of a clergyman, of Twick-

violent death in the very spring-time of his youth. Henry Mossop, one of the stateliest of stately actors, perishing, by slow degrees, of penury and grief, — which he bore in utter silence, — found a refuge, at last, in the gloomy barrenness of Chelsea Church. Theodore Hook, the cheeriest spirit of his time, the man who filled every hour of life with the sunshine of his wit, and was wasted and degraded by his own brilliancy, rests (close by Bishop Sherlock) in Fulham Churchyard, — one of the dreariest spots in the suburbs of London. Perhaps it does not much signify, when once the play is over, in what oblivion our crumbling relics are hidden away. Yet to most human creatures these are sacred things, and many a loving heart, for all

enham, and lived in the reign of William and Mary. Dramatic chronicles say that he was possessed of great talents as an actor, and of remarkable personal beauty. He was stabbed, in a quarrel, at the Rose Tavern; and after he had been laid out for the grave, such was the lively feminine interest in his handsome person, many ladies came, some masked and others openly, to view him in his shroud. This is mentioned in Colley Cibber's Apology. Charles Coffey, the dramatist, author of "The Devil upon Two Sticks," and other plays, lies in the vaults of St. Clement; as likewise does Thomas Rymer, historiographer for William III., successor to Shadwell, and author of "Fœdera," in seventeen volumes. In the church of St. Clement you may see the pew in which Dr. Johnson habitually sat, when he attended divine service there. It was his favourite church. The pew is in the gallery; and to those who honour the passionate integrity and fervent, devout zeal of the stalwart old champion of letters, it is indeed a sacred shrine.

time to come, will choose a consecrated spot for the repose of the dead, and will echo the tender words of Longfellow, — so truly expressive of a universal and reverent sentiment:

> " Take them, O grave, and let them lie
> Folded upon thy narrow shelves,
> As garments by the soul laid by
> And precious only to ourselves."

One of the pleasantest and saddest of the literary pilgrimages that I have made was that which brought me to the house in which Coleridge died, and the place where he was buried. The student needs not to be told that this poet, born in 1772, the year after Gray's death, bore the white lilies of pure literature till 1834, when he too entered into his rest. The last nineteen years of the life of Coleridge were spent in a house at Highgate; and here, within a few steps of each other, the visitor may behold his dwelling and his tomb. The house is one in a block of dwellings, situated in what is called The Grove — a broad and embowered street, a little way off from the centre of the village. There are gardens attached to these houses, both in the front and the rear, and the smooth and peaceful roadside walks in The Grove itself are pleasantly shaded by elms of noble size and abundant foliage. These were young trees when Coleridge saw them, and all this neighbourhood, in his day, was but thinly settled. Looking from his chamber window he could see the dusky outlines of sombre London, crowned with the dome of St. Paul's on the southern horizon, while, more near, across a fertile and smiling valley, the gray spire of Hampstead Church would bound his prospect, rising above the verdant woodland of Caen.[1] In front were beds of flowers, and all around he might hear the songs of birds that filled the fragrant air with their happy, careless music. Not far away stood the old church of Highgate, long since destroyed, in which he used to worship, and close by was the Gate House Inn, primitive, quaint, and cosey, which still is standing to comfort the weary traveller with its wholesome hospitality. Highgate, with all its rural peace, must have been a bustling place in the old times, for all the travel went through it that passed either into or out of London by the great north road, — that road in which Whittington heard the prophetic summons of the bells, and where may still be seen, suitably and rightly marked, the site of the stone on which he sat to rest. Here, indeed, the coaches used to halt, either to bait or to change horses, and here the many neglected little taverns still remaining, with their odd names and their swinging signs, testify to the discarded

[1] "Come in the first stage, so as either to walk or to be driven in Mr. Gilman's gig, to Caen wood and its delicious groves and alleys, the finest in England, a grand Cathedral aisle of giant lime-trees, Pope's favourite composition walk, when with the old Earl." — *Coleridge to Crabb Robinson. Highgate, June,* 1817.

customs of a by-gone age. Some years ago a new road was cut, so that travellers might wind around the hill, and avoid climbing the steep ascent to the village; and since then the grass has begun to grow in the streets. But such bustle as once enlivened the solitude of Highgate could never have been otherwise than agreeable diversion to its inhabitants; while for Coleridge himself, as we can well imagine, the London coach was welcome indeed, that brought to his door such well-loved friends as Charles Lamb, Joseph Henry Green, Crabb Robinson, Wordsworth, or Talfourd.

To this retreat the author of "The Ancient Mariner" withdrew in 1815, to live with his friend James Gilman, a surgeon, who had undertaken to rescue him from the demon of opium, but who, as De Quincey intimates, was lured by the poet into the service of the very fiend whom both had striven to subdue. It was his last refuge, and he never left it till he was released from life. As you ramble in this quiet neighbourhood your fancy will not fail to conjure up his placid figure,—the silver hair, the pale face, the great, luminous, changeful blue eyes, the somewhat portly form clothed in black raiment, the slow, feeble walk, the sweet, benignant manner, the voice that was. perfect melody, and the inexhaustible talk that was the flow of a golden sea of eloquence and wisdom. Coleridge was often seen walking here, with a book in his hand; and all the children of the village knew him and loved him. His presence is impressed forever upon this place, to haunt and to hallow it. He was a very great man. The wings of his imagination wave easily in the opal air of the highest heaven. The power and majesty of his thought are such as establish forever in the human mind the conviction of personal immortality. No man who reads Coleridge can doubt the destiny of the soul. Yet how forlorn the ending that this stately spirit was enforced to make! For more than thirty years he was the slave of opium. It broke up his home; it alienated his wife; it ruined his health; it made him utterly wretched. "I have been, through a large portion of my later life," he wrote, in 1834, "a sufferer, sorely afflicted with bodily pains, languor, and manifold infirmities." But back of all this, — more dreadful still and harder to bear, — was he not the slave of some ingrained perversity of the mind itself, some helpless and hopeless irresolution of character, some enervating spell of that sublime yet pitiable dejection of Hamlet, which kept him forever at war with himself, and, last of all, cast him out upon the homeless ocean of despair, to drift away into ruin and death! There are shapes more awful than his, in the records of literary history, — the ravaged, agonizing form of Swift, for instance, and the wonderful, desolate face of Byron; but there is no figure more forlorn and pathetic.

This way the memory of Coleridge came upon

me, standing at his grave. He should have been laid in some wild, free place, where the grass could grow above him and the trees could wave their branches over his head. They placed him in a ponderous tomb, of gray stone, in Highgate Churchyard, and, in later times, they have reared a new building above it, — the grammar school of the village, — so that now the tomb, fenced round with iron, is in a cold, barren, gloomy crypt, accessible, indeed, from the churchyard, through several arches, but grim and doleful in all its surroundings; as if the evil and cruel fate that marred his life were still triumphant over his ashes.

VII.

ON BARNET BATTLE-FIELD.

IN England, as elsewhere, every historic spot is occupied; and of course it sometimes happens, at such a spot, that its association is marred and its sentiment almost destroyed by the presence of the persons and the interests of to-day. The visitor to such places must carry with him not only knowledge and sensibility, but imagination and patience. He will not find the way strewn with roses nor the atmosphere of poetry ready-made for his enjoyment. That atmosphere, indeed, for the most part — especially in the cities — he must himself supply. Relics do not robe themselves for exhibition. The Past is utterly indifferent to its worshippers. All manner of little obstacles, too, will arise before the pilgrim, to thwart him in his search. The mental strain and bewilderment, the inevitable physical weariness, the soporific influence of the climate, the tumult of the streets, the frequent and disheartening spectacle of poverty, squalour, and vice, the capricious and untimely rain, the inconvenience of long distances, the ill-timed arrival and consequent disappointment, the occasional nervous sense of loneliness and insecurity, the inappropriate boor, the ignorant, garrulous porter, the extortionate cabman, and the jeering by-stander — all these must be regarded with resolute indifference by him who would ramble, pleasantly and profitably, in the footprints of English history. Everything depends, in other words, upon the eyes with which you observe, and the spirit which you impart. Never was a keener truth uttered than in the couplet of Wordsworth:

> "Minds that have nothing to confer
> Find little to perceive."

To the philosophic stranger, however, even this prosaic occupancy of historic places is not without its pleasurable, because humorous, significance. Such an observer in England will sometimes be amused as well as impressed by a sudden sense of the singular incidental position into which, — partly through the lapse of years and partly through a peculiarity of national character, — the scenes of famous events, not to say the events themselves, have gradually drifted. I thought of this one night, when, in Whitehall Gardens, I was looking at the statue of James the Second,—which there marks the place of the execution of his father, Charles the First,—and a courteous policeman came up and silently turned the light of his bull's-eye upon the inscription. A scene of more incongruous elements, or one suggestive of a more serio-comic contrast, could not be imagined. I thought of it again when standing on the village green near Barnet, and viewing, amid surroundings both pastoral and ludicrous, the column which there commemorates the defeat and death of the great Earl of Warwick, and, consequently, the final triumph of the Crown over the last of the Barons of England.

It was toward the close of a cool summer day, and of a long drive through the beautiful hedgerows of sweet and verdurous Middlesex, that I came to the villages of Barnet and Hadley, and went over the field of King Edward's victory,—that fatal, glorious field, on which Gloster showed such resolute valour, and where Neville, supreme and magnificent in disaster, fought on foot, to make sure that himself might go down in the stormy death of all his hopes. More than four hundred years have drifted by since that misty April morning when the star of Warwick was quenched in blood, and ten thousand men were slaughtered to end the strife between the Barons and the Crown; yet the results of that conflict are living facts in the government of England now, and in the fortunes of her inhabitants. If you were unaware of the solid simplicity and proud reticence of the English character, — leading it to merge all its shining deeds in one continuous fabric of achievement, like jewels set in a cloth of gold, — you might expect to find this spot adorned with a structure of more than common splendour. What you actually do find there is a plain monolith, standing in the middle of a common, at the junction of several roads, — the chief of which are those leading to Hatfield and St. Albans, in Hertfordshire, — and on one side of this column you may read, in letters of faded black, the comprehensive statement that "Here was fought the famous battle between Edward the Fourth and the Earl of Warwick, April 14th, anno 1471, in which the Earl was defeated and slain.[1]

In my reverie, standing at the foot of this humble, weather-stained monument, I saw the long range of Barnet Hills, mantled with grass and flowers and with the golden haze of a morning in spring, swarming with gorgeous horsemen and glittering with spears and banners; and I heard the vengeful clash of arms, the horrible neighing of maddened steeds, the furious shouts of onset, and all the nameless cries and groans of battle, commingled in a thrilling yet hideous din. Here rode King Edward, intrepid, handsome, and stalwart, with his proud, cruel smile and his long yellow hair. There

---

[1] The words "stick no bills" have been added, just below this inscription, with ludicrous effect.

Warwick swung his great two-handed sword, and mowed his foes like grain. And there the fiery form of Richard, splendid in burnished steel, darted like the scorpion, dealing death at every blow; till at last, in fatal mischance, the sad star of Oxford, assailed by its own friends, was swept out of the field, and the fight drove, raging, into the valleys of Hadley. How strangely, though, did this fancied picture contrast with the actual scene before me. At a little distance, all around the village green, the peaceful, embowered cottages kept their sentinel watch. Over the careless, straggling grass went the shadow of the passing clouds. Not a sound was heard, save the rustle of leaves and the low laughter of some little children, playing near the monument. Close by, and at rest, was a flock of geese, couched upon the cool earth, and, as their custom is, supremely contented with themselves and all the world. And at the very foot of the column, stretched out at his full length, in tattered garments that scarcely covered his nakedness, reposed the British labourer, fast asleep upon the sod. No more Wars of the Roses now; but calm retirement, smiling plenty, cool western winds, and sleep and peace —

> "With a red rose and a white rose
> Leaning, nodding at the wall."

VIII.

A GLIMPSE OF CANTERBURY.

ONE of the most impressive spots on earth, and one that especially teaches — with silent, pathetic eloquence and solemn admonition — the great lesson of contrast, the incessant flow of the ages and the inevitable decay and oblivion of the past, is the ancient city of Canterbury. Years and not merely days of residence here are essential to the adequate and right comprehension of this wonderful place. Yet even an hour passed among its shrines will teach you, as no printed word has ever taught, the measureless power and the sublime beauty of a perfect religious faith; while, as you stand and meditate in the shadow of the gray Cathedral walls, the pageant of a thousand years of history will pass before you like a dream. The city itself, with its bright, swift river (the Stour), its opulence of trees and flowers, its narrow, winding streets, its numerous antique buildings, its many towers, its fragments of ancient wall and gate, its formal decorations, its air of perfect cleanliness and thoughtful gravity, its beautiful, umbrageous suburbs, — where the scarlet of the poppies and the russet red of the clover make one vast rolling sea of colour and of fragrant delight, — and, to crown all, its stately character of wealth without ostentation and industry without tumult, must prove to you a deep and satisfying comfort. But, through all this, pervading and surmounting it all, the spirit of the place pours in upon your heart, and floods your whole being with the incense and organ music of passionate, jubilant devotion.

It was not superstition that reared those gorgeous fanes of worship which still adorn, even while they no longer consecrate, the ecclesiastic cities of the old world. In the days of Augustine, Dunstan, and Ethelnoth, humanity had begun to feel its profound and vital need of a sure and settled reliance on religious faith. The drifting spirit, worn with sorrow, doubt, and self-conflict, longed to be at peace — longed for a refuge equally from the evils and tortures of its own condition and the storms and perils of the world. In that longing it recognized its immortality and heard the voice of its Divine Parent; and out of the ecstatic joy and utter abandonment of its new-born, passionate, responsive faith, it built and consecrated those stupendous temples, — rearing them with all its love, no less than all its riches and all its power. There was no wealth that it would not give, no toil that it would not perform, and no sacrifice that it would not make, in the accomplishment of its sacred task. It was grandly, nobly, terribly in earnest, and it achieved a work that is not only sublime in its poetic majesty but measureless in the scope and extent of its moral and spiritual influence. It has left to succeeding ages not only a legacy of permanent beauty, not only a sublime symbol of religious faith, but an everlasting monument to the loveliness and greatness that are inherent in human nature. No creature with a human heart in his bosom can stand in such a building as Canterbury Cathedral without feeling a greater love and reverence than he ever felt before, alike for God and man.

On a day, this year, (July 27th, 1882), when a class of the boys of the King's School of Canterbury was graduated, the present writer chanced to be a listener to the impressive and touching sermon that was preached before them, in the chancel of the Cathedral; wherein they were tenderly admonished to keep unbroken their associations with their school-days, and to remember the lessons of the place itself. This counsel must have sunk deep into every mind. It is difficult to understand how any person reared amid such scenes and relics could ever cast away their hallowing influence. Even to the casual visitor the bare thought of the historic treasures that are garnered in this temple is, by itself, sufficient to implant in the bosom a memorable and lasting awe. For more than twelve hundred years the succession of the Archbishops of Canterbury has remained substantially unbroken. There have been ninety-three "primates of all England," of whom fifty-three were buried in the Cathedral, and here the tombs of fifteen of them are still visible. Here was buried the sagacious, crafty, inflexible, indomitable Henry the Fourth, — that Hereford whom Shakespeare has described and interpreted with matchless, immortal eloquence, — and here, cut off in the morning of his greatness, and lamented to this day in the hearts of the English people, was laid the body of Edward the Black Prince, who to a dauntless valour and terrible prowess in war added a high-souled, humane, and tender magnanimity in conquest, and whom personal virtues and shining public deeds united to make the ideal hero of chivalry. In no other way than by personal observance of such memorials can historic reading be invested with a perfect and permanent reality. Over the tomb of the Black Prince, with its fine recumbent effigy of gilded brass, hang the gauntlets that he wore; and they tell you that his sword formerly hung there, but that Oliver Cromwell, — who revealed his iconoclastic and unlovely character in making a stable of this Cathedral, — carried it away. Close at hand is the tomb of the wise, just, and gentle Cardinal Pole, simply inscribed, "Blessed are the dead which die in the Lord;" and you may touch a little, low mausoleum of gray stone, in which are the ashes of John Morton, that Bishop of Ely from whose garden in Holborn the strawberries were brought for the Duke of Gloster, on the day when he slaughtered the accomplished Hastings, and who "fled to Richmond," in good time, from the standard of the grisly and dangerous Protector. Standing there, I could almost hear the resolute, scornful voice of Richard, breathing out, in clear, implacable accents:

> "Morton with Richmond touches me more near
> Than Buckingham and his rash-levied numbers."

The astute Morton, when Bosworth was over, and Richmond had assumed the crown, and Bourchier had died, was made Archbishop of Canterbury; and as such, at a great age, he passed away. A few hundred yards from his place of rest, in a vault beneath the Church of St. Dunstan, is the head of Sir Thomas More (the body being in St. Peter's, at the Tower of London), who, in his youth, had been a member of Morton's ecclesiastical household, and whose greatness that prelate had foreseen and prophesied. Did no shadow of the scaffold ever fall across the statesman's thoughts, as he looked upon that handsome, manly boy, and thought of the troublous times that were raging about them? Morton, aged ninety, died in 1500; More, aged fifty-five, in 1535. Strange fate, indeed, was that, and as inscrutable as mournful, which gave to those who in life had been like father and son such a ghastly association in death![1] They show you, of course, the spot where Becket was murdered, and the stone steps, worn hollow by the thousands upon thousands of devout pilgrims who, in the days before the Reformation, crept up to weep and pray at the costly, resplendent shrine of St. Thomas. The bones of Becket, as all the world knows, were, by command of Henry the Eighth, burnt, and scattered to the winds, while his shrine was pillaged and destroyed. Neither tomb nor scutcheon commemorates him here, — but the Cathedral itself is his monument. There it stands, with its grand columns and glorious arches, its towers of enormous size and its long vistas of distance so mysterious and awful, its gloomy crypt

[1] St. Dunstan's Church was connected with the Convent of St. Gregory. The Roper family, in the time of Henry the Fourth, founded a chapel in it, in which are two marble tombs, commemorative of them, and underneath which is their burial vault. Margaret Roper, Sir Thomas More's daughter, obtained her father's head, after his execution, and buried it here. The vault was opened in 1835, — when a new pavement was laid in the chancel of this church, — and persons descending into it saw the head, in a leaden box shaped like a bee-hive, open in front, set in a niche in the wall, and faced with an iron grating.

where once the silver lamps sparkled and the smoking censers were swung, its tombs of mighty warriors and statesmen, its frayed and crumbling banners, and the eternal, majestic silence with which it broods over the love, ambition, glory, defeat, and anguish of a thousand years, dissolved now and ended in a little dust! As the organ music died away I looked upward and saw where a bird was wildly flying to and fro through the vast spaces beneath its lofty roof, in the vain effort to find some outlet of escape. Fit emblem, truly, of the human mind which strives to comprehend and to utter the meaning of this marvellous fabric!

IX.

THE SHRINES OF WARWICKSHIRE.

NIGHT, in Stratford-on-Avon — a summer night, with large, solemn stars, a cool and fragrant breeze and the stillness of perfect rest. From this high and grassy bank I look forth across the darkened meadows and the smooth and shining river, and see the little town where it lies asleep. Hardly a light is anywhere visible. A few great elms, near by, are nodding and rustling in the wind, and once or twice a drowsy bird-note floats up from the neighbouring thicket that skirts the vacant, lonely road. There, at some distance, are the dim arches of Clopton's Bridge. In front — a graceful, shapely mass, indistinct in the starlight — rises the fair Memorial, Stratford's honour and pride. Further off, glimmering through the tree-tops, is the dusky spire of Trinity, keeping its sacred vigil over the dust of Shakespeare. Nothing here is changed. The same tranquil beauty, as of old, hallows this place; the same sense of awe and mystery broods over its silent shrines of everlasting renown. Long and weary the years have been since last I saw it; but to-night they are remembered only as a fleeting and troubled dream. Here, once more, is the highest and noblest companionship this world can give. Here, once more, is the almost visible presence of the one magician who can lift the soul out of the infinite weariness of common things, and give it strength and peace. The old time has come back, and the bloom of the heart that I thought had all faded and gone. I stroll again to the river's brink, and take my place in the boat, and, trailing my hand in the dark waters of Avon, forget every trouble that ever I have known.

It is often said, with reference to memorable places, that the best view always is the first view. No doubt the accustomed eye sees blemishes. No doubt the supreme moments of human life are few, and come but once; and neither of them is ever repeated. Yet frequently it will be found that the change is in ourselves and not in the objects we behold. Scott has glanced at this truth, in a few mournful lines, written toward the close of his heroic and beautiful life. Here at Stratford, however, I am not conscious that the wonderful charm of the place is in any degree impaired. The town still preserves its old-fashioned air, its quaintness, its perfect cleanliness and order. At the Shakespeare cottage, in the stillness of the room where he was born, the spirits of mystery and reverence still keep their imperial state. At the ancient Grammar School, with its pent-house roof and its dark, sagging rafters, you still may see, in fancy, the unwilling schoolboy gazing upward absently at the great, rugged timbers, or looking wistfully at the sunshine, where it streams through the little lattice windows of his prison. New Place, with its lovely lawn, its spacious gardens, the ancestral mulberry and the ivy-covered well, will bring the poet before you, as he lived and moved in the meridian of his greatness. "Cymbeline," "The Tempest" and "A Winter's Tale," the last of his works, undoubtedly were written here; and this alone should make it a hallowed spot. Here he blessed his young daughter on her wedding day; here his eyes closed in the last long sleep; and from this place he was carried to his grave in the chancel of Stratford Church. I pass once again through the fragrant avenue of limes, the silent churchyard with its crumbling monuments, the dim porch, the twilight of the venerable temple, and kneel at last above the ashes of Shakespeare. What majesty in this triumphant rest! All the great labor accomplished. The universal human heart interpreted with a living voice. The memory and the imagination of mankind stored forever with words of sublime eloquence and images of immortal beauty. The noble lesson of self-conquest — the lesson of the entire adequacy of the resolute, virtuous, patient human will — set forth so grandly that all the world must see its meaning and marvel at its splendour. And, last of all, death itself shorn of its terrours, and made a trivial thing.

There is a new custodian at New Place, and, upon the receipt of a sixpence, he will show you the little museum that is kept there — including the shovelboard from the old Falcon tavern across the way, on which the poet himself might have played — and he will lead you through the gardens, and descant on the mulberry and on the ancient and still unforgiven vandalism of the Rev. Francis Gastrell, by whom the Shakespeare mansion was destroyed (1757), and will pause at the well, and at the fragments of the foundation, covered now with stout screens of wire gauze. There is a fresh and fragrant beauty all about these grounds, an atmosphere of sunshine, life, comfort and elegance of state, that no observer can miss. This same keeper also has the keys of the Guild Chapel, opposite, on which Shakespeare looked from his windows and his garden, and in which he was the holder of two sittings. You will enter it by the same porch through which he walked, and see the arch and columns and tall, transomed windows on which his gaze has often rested. The interior is cold and barren now, for the Scriptural wall-paintings, discovered here in 1804, under thick coatings of whitewash, have been removed or have faded, and the wooden pews, which apparently are modern, have not yet been embrowned by age. Yet this church, known beyond question as one of Shakespeare's personal haunts, will hold you with the strongest tie of reverence and sympathy. The Falcon tavern, near by, though furnished now with a new front, is the same that he frequented three hundred years ago. At his birthplace everything remains unchanged. The gentle old ladies who have so long guarded and shown it still have it in their affectionate care. The ceiling of the room in which the poet was born — that room which contains "the Actors' Pillar" and the thousands of signatures on walls and windows — is slowly crumbling to pieces. Every morning many little particles of the plaster are found upon the floor. The area of tiny, delicate laths, to sustain this ceiling has more than doubled since I last saw it, five years ago. It was on the ceiling that Lord Byron wrote his name, but this has flaked off and disappeared. In the museum hall, once the Swan Inn, they are forming a library; and here, among many objects of dubious value, you may see at least one Shakespearean relic of extraordinary interest. This is the MS. letter of Richard Quiney — whose son became in 1616 the husband of Shakespeare's youngest daughter, Judith — asking the poet for the loan of thirty pounds. It is enclosed between plates of glass in a frame, and usually kept covered with a cloth, so that the sunlight may not fade the ink; and the window opposite to which it is placed, at right angles to the casement, is protected by a gauze of wire from danger of the accidental missile. The date of this letter is October 25, 1598, and thirty English pounds then was a sum equivalent to about six hundred dollars of American money now. This is the only letter known to be in existence that Shakespeare received. The elder of the ladies who keep this house will recite to you its text, from memory — giving a delicious old-fashioned flavour to its quaint phraseology and fervent spirit, as rich and strange as the odour of the wild thyme and rosemary that grow in her garden beds. This antique touch adds a wonderful charm to the relics of the past. I found it once more when sitting in the chimney-corner of Anne Hathaway's kitchen; and again in the lovely little church at Charlcote, where a simple, kindly woman, not ashamed to reverence the place and the dead, stood with me at the tomb of the Lucys, and repeated from memory the tender, sincere, and eloquent epitaph with which Sir Thomas Lucy thereon commemorates his wife. The lettering is small and indistinct on the tomb, but, having often read it, I well knew how correctly it was then spoken. Nor shall I ever read it again without thinking of that low and pleasant voice, the hush of the beautiful church, the afternoon sunlight streaming through the oriel window, and — visible through the doorway arch — the roses waving among the churchyard graves.

In the days of Shakespeare's courtship, when he strolled across the fields to Anne Hathaway's cottage at Shottery, his path, we may be sure, ran through wild pasture land and tangled thicket. A fourth part of England at that time was a wilderness, and the entire population of that country did not exceed five millions of persons. The Stratford-on-Avon of to-day is still possessed of many of its ancient features; but the region round about it then must have been rude and wild, in comparison with what it is at present. If you take the footpath to Shottery now you will pass between low fences and along the margin of gardens, — now in the sunshine, and now in the shadow of larch and elm, while the sweet air blows upon your face and the expeditious rook makes rapid wing to the woodland, cawing as he flies. In the old cottage, with its roof of thatch, its crooked rafters, its odorous hedges and climbing vines, its leafy well and its tangled garden, everything remains the same. Mrs. Mary Taylor Baker, the last living descendant of the Hathaways, born in this house, always a resident here, and now an elderly woman, still has it in her keeping, and still displays to you the ancient carved bedstead in the garret, the wooden settle by the kitchen fireside, the hearth at which Shakespeare sat, the great blackened chimney with its adroit iron "fish-back" for the better regulation of the tea-kettle, and the brown and tattered Bible with the Hathaway family record. Sitting in an old arm-chair, in the corner of Anne Hathaway's bedroom, I could hear in the perfumed summer stillness, the low twittering of birds, whose nest is in the covering thatch, and whose songs would awaken the sleeper at the earliest light of dawn. A better idea can be obtained in this cottage than in either the birthplace or any other Shakespearean haunt of what the real life actually was of the common people of England in Shakepeare's day. The stone floor and oaken timbers of the Hathaway kitchen, stained and darkened in the slow decay of three hundred years, have lost no particle of their pristine character. The occupant of the cottage has not been absent from it more than a week during upward of half a century. In such a nook the inherited habits of living do not alter. "The thing that has been is the thing that shall be," and the customs of long ago are the customs of to-day.

The Red Horse Inn is in new hands now, and seems to be fresher and brighter than of old—without, however, having parted with either its antique furniture or its delightful antique ways. The old mahogany and wax-candle period has not ended yet, in this happy place, and you sink to sleep on a snow-white pillow, soft as down and fragrant as lavender. One important change is especially to be remarked. They have made a niche in the right-hand corner of Washington Irving's parlour, and in it have placed his arm-chair, recushioned and polished, and sequestered from touch by a large sheet of plate-glass. The relic may still be seen, but the pilgrim can sit upon it no more. Perhaps it might be well to enshrine "Geoffrey Crayon's Sceptre" in a somewhat similar way. It could be fastened to a shield, displaying the American colours, and hung up in this storied little room. At present it is the tenant of a muslin bag and keeps its state in the seclusion of a bureau drawer; nor is it shown except upon request — like the beautiful marble statue of Donne, in his shroud, niched in the chancel wall of St. Paul's Cathedral.

One of the strongest instincts of the English character is the instinct of permanence. It acts involuntarily, it pervades the national life, and, as Pope said of the universal soul, it operates unspent. Institutions seem to have grown out of human nature in this country, and are as much its expression as blossoms, leaves, and flowers are the expression of inevitable law. A custom, in England, once established, is seldom or never changed. The brilliant career, the memorable achievement, the great character, once fulfilled, takes a permanent shape in some kind of outward and visible memorial, some absolute and palpable fact, which thenceforth is an accepted part of the history of the land and the experience of its people. England means stability — the fireside and the altar, home here and heaven hereafter; and this is the secret of the power that she wields in the affairs of the world and the charm that she diffuses over the domain of thought. Such a temple as St. Paul's Cathedral, such a palace as Hampton Court, such a castle as that of Windsor or that of Warwick, is the natural, spontaneous expression of the English instinct of permanence; and it is in memorials like these that England has written her history, with symbols that can perish only with time itself. At intervals her latent animal ferocity breaks loose — as it did under Henry the Eighth, under Mary, under Cromwell, and under James the Second, — and for a brief time ramps and bellows, striving to deface and deform the surrounding structure of beauty that has been slowly and painfully reared out of her deep heart and her sane civilization. But the tears of human pity soon quench the fires of Smithfield, and it is only for a little while that the Puritan soldiers play at nine-pins in the nave of St. Paul's. This fever of animal impulse, this wild revolt of petulant impatience, is soon cooled; and then the great work goes on again, as calmly and surely as before — that great work of educating mankind to the level of constitutional liberty, in which England has been engaged for well nigh a thousand years, and in which the American Republic, though sometimes at variance with her methods and her spirit, is, nevertheless, her follower and the consequence of her example. Our Declaration was made in 1776: the Declaration to the Prince of Orange is dated 1689, and the Bill of Rights in 1628, while Magna Charta was secured in 1215.

Throughout every part of this sumptuous and splendid domain of Warwickshire the symbols of English stability and the relics of historic times are numerous and deeply impressive. At Stratford the reverence of the nineteenth century takes its practical, substantial form, not alone in the honourable preservation of the ancient Shakespearean shrines, but in the Shakespeare Memorial. This noble fabric, though mainly due to the fealty of England, is also, to some extent, representative of the practical sympathy of America. Several Americans — Edwin Booth, Herman Vezin, M. D. Conway, and W. H. Reynolds among them — are contributors to the fund that built it, and an American gentlewoman, Miss Kate Field, has worked for its cause with excellent zeal, untiring fidelity, and good results. The work is not yet finished. About £2,000 will be required to complete the tower and suitably decorate the interior. But already it is a noble monument. It stands upon the margin of the Avon, not a great way off from the Church of the Holy Trinity, which is Shakespeare's grave; so that these two buildings are the conspicuous points of the landscape, and seem to confront each other with sympathetic greeting, as if conscious of their sacred trust. The vacant land adjacent, extending both ways between the road and the river, is a part of the Memorial estate, and is to be converted into a park, with winding pathways and abundance of shade-trees and of flowers,—by means of which the prospect will be made still fairer than now it is, and will be kept forever unbroken between the Memorial and the Church. Under this ample Tudor roof — so stately and yet so meek and quaint — are already united a theatre, a library, and a hall of pictures. The theatre, as yet, lacks requisite ornament. Except for a gay drop-curtain, illustrating the processional progress of Queen Elizabeth when "going to the Globe Theatre," it is barren of colour; while its divisions of seats are in conformity with the inconvenient arrangements of the common London theatre of to-day. Queen Elizabeth heard plays in the Hall of the Middle Temple, the Hall of Hampton Palace, and at Greenwich and Richmond; but she never went to the Globe Theatre. In historic temples there should be no trifling with historic themes; and surely, in a theatre of the nineteenth century, dedicated to Shakespeare, while no fantastic regard should be paid to the usages of the past, it would be tasteful and proper to blend the best of ancient ways with all the luxury and elegance of these times. It is much, however, to have built what can readily be made a lovely theatre; and meanwhile, through the affectionate generosity of friends in all parts of the world, the Library shelves are continually gathering treasures, and the Hall of Paintings is growing more and more the imposing and beautiful expository that it was intended to be of Shakespearean poetry and the history of the English stage. Many faces of actors appear upon these walls — from Garrick to Edmund Kean, from Macready to Henry Irving, from Kemble to Edwin Booth, from Mrs. Siddons to Mary Anderson. Prominent among the pictures is the famous portrait of Garrick and his wife, playing at cards, wherein the lovely laughing lady archly discloses that her hands are full of hearts. Not otherwise, truly, is it with sweet and gentle Stratford herself, where peace and beauty and the most hallowed and hallowing of poetic associations garner up, forever and forever, the hearts of all mankind.

In previous papers upon this subject (published in " The Trip to England," 1878–1881), I have tried to express the feelings that are aroused by personal contact with the relics of Shakespeare — the objects which he saw and the fields through which he wandered. Fancy would never tire of lingering in this delicious region of flowers and of dreams. From the hideous vileness of the social condition of London in the time of James the First, Shakespeare must indeed have rejoiced to depart into this blooming garden of rustic tranquillity. Here also he could find the surroundings that were needful to sustain him amid the vast and overwhelming labours of his final period. No man, however great his powers, can ever, in this world, escape from the trammels under which nature enjoins and permits the exercise of the brain. Ease, in the intellectual life, is always visionary. The higher a man's faculties the higher are his ideals, — toward which, under the operation of a divine law, he must perpetually strive, but to the height of which he will never absolutely attain. So, inevitably, it was with Shakespeare. But, although genius cannot escape from itself, and is no more free than the humblest toiler in the vast scheme of creation, it may — and it must — sometimes escape from the world : and this wise poet, of all men else, would surely recognize and strongly grasp the great privilege of solitude amidst the sweetest and most soothing adjuncts of natural beauty. That privilege he found in the sparkling and fragrant gardens of Warwick, the woods and fields and waters of Avon, where he had played as a boy, and where love had laid its first kiss upon his lips, and poetry first opened upon his inspired vision the eternal glories of her celestial world. It still abides there, for every gentle soul that can feel its influence — to deepen the glow of noble passion, to soften the sting of grief, and to touch the lips of worship with a fresh sacrament of patience and beauty.

X.

A BORROWER OF THE NIGHT.

*"I must become a borrower of the night,
For a dark hour or twain."* MACBETH.

MIDNIGHT has just sounded from the tower of St. Martin's Church. It is a peaceful night, faintly lit with stars, and in the region round about Trafalgar Square a dream-like stillness broods over the darkened city, now slowly hushing itself to its brief and troubled rest. This is the centre of the heart of modern civilization, the very middle of the greatest city in the world — the vast, seething alembic of a grand future, the stately monument of a deathless past. Here, alone, in my quiet room of this old English inn, let me meditate awhile on some of the scenes that are near me — the strange, romantic, sad, grand objects that I have seen, the memorable figures of beauty, genius, and renown that haunt this classic land.

How solemn and awful now must be the gloom within the walls of the Abbey. A walk of only a few minutes would bring me to its gates — the gates of the most renowned mausoleum on earth. No human foot to-night invades its sacred precincts. The dead alone possess it. I see, upon its gray walls, the marble figures, white and spectral, staring through the darkness. I hear the night-wind moaning around its lofty towers and faintly sobbing in the dim, mysterious spaces beneath its fretted roof. Here and there a ray of starlight, streaming through the sumptuous rose window, falls and lingers, in ruby or emerald gleam, on tomb, or pillar, or dusky pavement. Rustling noises, vague and fearful, float from those dim chapels where the great kings lie in state, with marble effigies recumbent above their bones. At such an hour as this, in such a place, do the dead come out of their graves? The resolute, implacable Queen Elizabeth, the beautiful, wretched Queen of Scots, the two royal boys murdered in the Tower, Charles the Merry and William the Silent — are these, and such as these, among the phantoms that fill the haunted aisles? What a wonderful company it would be, for human eyes to behold! And with what passionate love or hatred, what amazement, or what haughty scorn, its members would look upon each other's faces, in this miraculous meeting! Here, through the glimmering, icy waste, would pass before the watcher the august shades of the poets of five hundred years. Now would glide the ghosts of Chaucer, Spenser, Jonson, Beaumont, Dryden, Cowley, Congreve, Addison, Prior, Campbell, Garrick, Burke, Sheridan, Newton, and Macaulay — children of divine genius, that here mingled with the earth. The grim Edward, who so long ravaged Scotland; the blunt, chivalrous Henry, who conquered France; the lovely, lamentable victim at Pomfret, and the harsh, haughty, astute victor at Bosworth; James with his babbling tongue, and William with his impassive, predominant visage — they would all mingle with the spectral multitude, and vanish into the gloom. Gentler faces, too, might here once more reveal their loveliness and their grief — Eleanor de Bohun, broken-hearted for her murdered lord; Elizabeth Claypole, the meek, merciful, beloved daughter of Cromwell; Matilda, Queen to Henry the First, and model of every grace and virtue; and poor Anne Nevil, destroyed by the baleful passion of Gloster. Strange sights, truly, in the lonesome Abbey to-night!

In the sombre crypt beneath St. Paul's Cathedral, how thrilling now must be the heavy stillness. No sound can enter there. No breeze from the upper world can stir the dust upon those massive sepulchres. Even in day-time that shadowy vista, with its groined arches, and the black tombs of Wellington and Nelson, and the ponderous funeral-car of the Iron Duke, is seen with a shudder. How strangely, how fearfully the mind would be impressed, of him who should wander there to-night! What sublime reflections would be his, standing beside the ashes of the great Admiral, and thinking of that fiery, dauntless spirit — so simple, resolute, and true — who made the earth and the seas alike resound with the splendid tumult of his deeds. Somewhere beneath this pavement is the dust of Sir Philip Sidney — buried here before the destruction of the old cathedral, in the great fire of 1666 — and here, too, is the nameless grave of the mighty Duke of Lancaster, John of Gaunt. Shakespeare was only twenty-two years old when Sidney fell, at the battle of Zutphen, and, being then resident in London, he might readily have seen, and doubtless did see, the splendid funeral procession with which the body of that heroic gentleman — radiant and immortal example of perfect chivalry — was borne to the tomb. Hither came Henry of Hereford — returning from exile and deposing the handsome, visionary, useless Richard — to mourn over the relics of his father, dead of sorrow for his son's absence and his country's shame. Here, at the venerable age of ninety-one, the glorious brain of Wren found rest at last, beneath the stupendous temple that himself had reared. The watcher in the crypt to-night would see, perchance, or fancy that he saw, these figures from the storied past. Beneath this roof—the soul and the perfect symbol of sublimity!—are ranged more than fourscore monuments to heroic martial persons who have died for England, by land or sea. Here, too, are gathered, in everlasting repose, the honoured relics of men who were famous in the arts of peace. Reynolds and Opie, Lawrence and West, Landseer, Turner, Cruikshank, and many more, sleep under the sculptured pavement where now the pilgrim walks. For fifteen centuries a Christian church has stood upon this spot, and through it has poured, with organ strains and glancing lights, an endless procession of prelates and statesmen, of poets and warriors and kings. Surely this is hallowed and haunted ground! Surely to him the spirits of the mighty dead would be very near, who—alone, in the darkness—should stand to-night within those sacred walls, and hear, beneath that awful dome, the mellow thunder of the bells of God.

How looks, to-night, the interior of the chapel of the Foundling Hospital? Dark and lonesome, no doubt, with its heavy galleries and sombre pews, and the great organ—Handel's gift—standing there, mute and grim, between the ascending tiers of empty seats. But never, in my remembrance, will it cease to present a picture more impressive and touching than words can say. At least three hundred children, rescued from shame and penury by this noble benevolence, were ranged around that organ when I saw it, and, in their artless, frail little voices, singing a hymn of praise and worship. Well nigh one hundred and fifty years have passed since this grand institution of charity — the sacred work and blessed legacy of Captain Thomas Coram — was established in this place. What a divine good it has accomplished, and continues to accomplish, and what a pure glory hallows its founder's name! Here the poor mother, betrayed and deserted, may take her child, and find for it a safe and happy home, and a chance in life — nor will she herself be turned adrift without sympathy and help. The poet and novelist, George Croly, was once chaplain of the Foundling Hospital, and he preached some noble sermons there; but these were thought to be above the comprehension of his usual audience, and he presently resigned the place. It was an aged clergyman who preached there within my hearing, and I remember he consumed the most part of an hour in saying that a good way in which to keep the tongue from speaking evil is to keep the heart kind and pure. Better than any sermon, though, was the spectacle of those poor children, rescued out of their helplessness and reared in comfort and affection. Several fine works of art are owned by this hospital and shown to visitors — paintings by Gainsborough and Reynolds, and a portrait of Captain Coram, by Hogarth. May the turf lie lightly on him, wheresoever he rests, and daisies and violets deck his hallowed grave!

No man ever did a better deed than he, and the darkest night that ever was cannot darken his fame.

How dim and silent now are all those narrow and dingy little streets and lanes around Paul's Churchyard and the Temple, where Johnson and Goldsmith loved to ramble! More than once have I wandered there, in the late hours of the night, meeting scarce a human creature, but conscious of a royal company indeed, of the wits and poets and players of a far-off time. Darkness now, on busy Smithfield, where once the frequent, cruel flames of bigotry shed forth a glare that sickened the light of day. Murky and grim enough to-night is that grand processional walk in St. Bartholomew's Chapel, where the great gray pillars and splendid Norman arches of the twelfth century are mouldering in neglect and decay. Sweet to fancy and dear in recollection, the old church comes back to me now, with the sound of children's voices and the wail of the organ strangely breaking on its pensive rest. Stillness and peace over arid Bunhill Fields — the last haven of many a Puritan worthy, and hallowed to many a pilgrim as the resting-place of Bunyan and of Watts. In many a park and gloomy square the watcher now would hear only a rustling of leaves or the fretful twitter of half-awakened birds. Around Primrose Hill and out toward Hampstead many a night-walk have I taken, that seemed like rambling in a desert — so dark and still are the walled houses, so perfect is the solitude. In Drury Lane, even at this late hour, there would be some movement; but cold and dense as ever the shadows are resting on that little graveyard, behind it, where Lady Dedlock went to die. The place, it is a comfort to know, has been cleaned, of late, and is now decent and in order — as all such places should be. To walk in Bow Street now, — might it not be to meet the shades of Waller and Wycherly and Betterton, who lived and died there; to have a greeting from the silver-tongued Barry; or to see, in draggled lace and ruffles, the stalwart figure and flushed and roystering countenance of Henry Fielding? Very quiet now are those grim stone chambers in the terrible Tower of London, where so many tears have fallen and so many noble hearts been split with sorrow. Does Brackenbury still kneel in the cold, lonely, and vacant chapel of St. John; or the sad ghost of Monmouth hover in the chancel of St. Peter's? How sweet to-night would be the rustle of the ivy on the dark walls of Hadley Church, where so lately I breathed the rose-scented air and heard the warbling thrush, and blessed, with a grateful heart, the loving-kindness that makes such beauty in the world. Out there on the hill-side of Highgate, populous with death, the starlight gleams on many a ponderous tomb and the white marble of many a sculptured statue, where dear and famous names will lure the traveller's footsteps, for years to come. There

Lyndhurst rests, in honour and peace, and there is hushed the tuneful voice of Dempster — never to be heard any more, either when snows are flying, or "when green leaves come again." Not many days have passed since I stood there, by the humble gravestone of poor Charles Harcourt, and remembered all the gentle enthusiasm with which, five years ago (1877), he spoke to me of the character of *Jacques* — which he loved — and how well he repeated the immortal lines upon the drama of human life. For him the "strange, eventful history" came early and suddenly to an end. May peace be with him — who here made only comfort and joy for all around him! In this ground, too, I saw the sculptured medallion of the well-beloved George Honey — "all his frolics o'er," and nothing left but this. Many a golden moment did we have, old friend, and by me thou art not forgotten! The lapse of a few years changes the whole face of life; but nothing can ever take from us our memories of the past. Here, around me, in the still watches of the night, are the faces that will never smile again, and the voices that will speak no more — Sothern, with his silvery hair and bright and kindly smile, from that crowded corner of the little churchyard of Southampton; and droll Harry Beckett, and poor Adelaide Neilson, from the dismal cemetery of Brompton. And if I look from yonder window I shall not see either the lions of Landseer or the homeless and vagrant wretches who sleep around them; but high in her silver chariot, surrounded with all the pomp and splendour that royal England knows, and marching to her coronation in Westminster Abbey, the beautiful figure of Anne Boleyn, with her dark eyes full of triumph, and her mane of golden hair flashing in the sun. On this spot is written the whole history of a mighty empire. Here are garnered up such loves and hopes, such memories and sorrows, as never can be spoken. Pass, ye shadows! Let the night wane and the morning break.

IN MEMORY OF LONGFELLOW.
1882.

I.

THE POET'S DEATH.

THE fact of Longfellow's death comes home to hundreds of hearts with a sense of personal loss and bereavement. The lovable quality in his writings, which was the natural and spontaneous reflex of the gentle tenderness of his nature, had endeared him not less as a man than as a poet. To read him was to know him, and, as Halleck said of Drake, to know him was to love him; so that his readers were, in fact, his affectionate friends. The reading of Longfellow is like sitting by the fireside of a sympathetic and cherished companion. The atmosphere of his works has the refinement and elegance of a sumptuous and well-ordered library; but also it has the soft tranquillity and smiling contentment of a happy home.

To any one who ever was, in fact, privileged to sit by the fireside of the poet, the thought that he is lying there in death is almost inconceivable, and brings with it an overwhelming solemnity. No man ever diffused around himself a more radiant influence of life, cheerfulness, and vigorous hope than Longfellow did, beneath his own roof. He was not, indeed, a demonstrative person; he did not overflow with effusion, or cover by a boisterous heartiness the absence of a sincere welcome. But he never failed to do the right thing in the right way, or to say the right word at the right time. He was thoughtful for every one who approached him. He knew by unerring intuition the ways of true grace — which flow out of true kindness. He was entirely frank and simple, bearing himself always with gentle dignity, and speaking always with a quiet sweetness that was inexpressibly winning. With youth in particular he had a profound and comprehensive sympathy. He understood all its ardours and aspirations, its confusion in presence of the mysteries of life, its embarrassments amid unfamiliar surroundings, its craving for recognition, its sensitive heart, and its dream-like spirit. "The thoughts of youth are long, long thoughts." To the last day of his life he carried this mood of youth; and no one ever heard from his lips a word of satire or discouragement. His first and greatest impulse was sympathy. In domestic life this displayed itself in a constant, unobtrusive solicitude for the comfort of all around him, and in a thousand little courtesies which equally adorned his conduct and comforted his associates. In his writings it is the lambent flame of every page.

Yet there was no element of insipidity in his character. If he preferred always to see the most agreeable side, and to speak always the most agreeable word, it was not that he was blind to defects, or assiduous to please, or insincere, or acquisitive of popularity. When occasion required it he spoke his convictions, whether acceptable or otherwise, fully and firmly, and he could rebuke injustice or ill-breeding with a cool censure that was all the more implacable for its calmness and reserve. He never obtruded his scholarship, but if the drift of conversation carried him that way, he tinted his discourse with many a shining ray of knowledge and many a coloured flash of anecdote, with citations from a wide range of books, and with a peculiar, dry, half-veiled drollery that was kindly, mischievous, and delightfully pungent. His tolerance was neither a weakness nor an artifice: it was the outgrowth of constitutional charity and tenderness toward that human nature of which he possessed so much, and which he knew so well.

Those who remember him in early years say that he was remarkable for personal beauty and for the perfect order and refinement of his life and manners. From the first he seems to have possessed the composure of high poetic genius.

Those who think that he was passionless, and that he knew little or nothing of tragedy, must have read to but little purpose such poems as "The Goblet of Life," "The Light of Stars," or the closing chapters of "Hyperion." Even his familiar ballad of "The Bridge" is eloquent of a profound knowledge of grief; and it may be doubted whether our language contains a more absolute poetic note of anguish and fortitude — when one considers its bleak isolation and its mournful significance — than his lines called "Weariness." He was not a Byron. His poetry is not the poetry of storm and stress. The "banner, torn but flying," which "streams like a thunder-storm against the wind," is nowhere unfurled in all his writings. But, if he did not utter the conflict, he clearly and sweetly uttered the consciousness of it, and the grand clarion note of patience and conquest. Of the trials and cares that are common to humanity, and that can be named and known, he had his share; but also he had the experience which the poetic nature invariably and inevitably draws upon itself. He had felt all that Burns felt, in writing "To Mary in Heaven." He had felt all that Goethe felt, in writing that wonderful passage of "Faust" which ends with the curse on patience as the worst of our human afflictions. But he would suffer no shock of sorrow to turn his life into a delirium. He would meet every trouble as a man ought to meet it who believes in the immortal destiny of the human soul. When he lost, under circumstances so pathetic and tragical, twenty years ago (1861), the wife whom he so entirely loved (that beautiful and stately lady, whom to remember is to wonder that so much loveliness and worth could take a mortal shape), he took the terrible anguish into the silent chambers of his own heart, he bore it with unflinching and uncomplaining fortitude; and from that day to this, no reader of his writings has been visited with one repining murmur, one plea for sympathy, one wail of personal loneliness or despondency or misanthropical bitterness. All that was ever shown of that misery was the simple grandeur of endurance combined with even a more wistful and readier and deeper sympathy with the sorrows of mankind.

There are poets, and good ones too, who seem never to get beyond the necessity of utterance for their own sake. Longfellow was not an egotist. He thought of others; and the permanent value of his writings consists in this — that he helped to utter the emotions of the universal human heart. It is when a writer speaks for us what were else unspoken — setting our minds free and giving us strength to meet the cares of life and the hour of death — that he first becomes of any real value. Longfellow has done this for thousands of human beings, and done it in that language of perfect simplicity — never bald, never insipid, never failing to exalt the subject — which is at once the most beautiful and the most difficult of all the elements of literature. And the high thoughts and tender feelings that he has thus spoken, the limpid, soft, and tranquil strain of his music — breathing out so truly our home loves, our tender longing for those that are dead and gone, the trust that we all would cherish in a happy future beyond the grave, the purpose to work nobly and endure bravely while we live — will sound on in the ears of the world, long after every hand and heart that honours him or grieves for him to-day is mouldering in the dust.

II.

PERSONAL RECOLLECTIONS.

THE least of us who have recollections of such a man as Longfellow may surely venture, now, to add them to the general stock of knowledge, without incurring the reproach of intrusiveness. My remembrance of him goes back to a period about thirty years ago, when he was a professor in Harvard University. I had read every line he had then published, and such was the affection he inspired, even in a boyish mind, that on many a summer night I walked several miles, to his house, only to put my hand upon the latch of his gate, which he himself had touched. More than any one else among the many famous persons whom, since then, it has been my fortune to know, he aroused this feeling of mingled tenderness and reverence. I saw him often — walking in the streets of Cambridge or looking at the books, in the old shop of Ticknor and Fields, at the corner of Washington and School Streets, in Boston — long before I was honoured with his personal acquaintance; and I observed him closely — as a youth naturally observes the object of his honest admiration. His dignity and grace, and the beautiful refinement of his countenance, together with his perfect taste in dress and the exquisite simplicity of his manners, made him the absolute ideal of what a poet should be. His voice, too, was soft, sweet, and musical, and, like his face, it had the innate charm of tranquillity. His eyes were blue-gray, very bright and brave, changeable under the influence of emotion (as, afterward, I often saw), but mostly calm, grave, attentive, and gentle. The habitual expression of his face was not that of sadness; and yet it was pensive. Perhaps it may be best described as that of serious and tender thoughtfulness. He had conquered his own sorrows, thus far, but the sorrows of others threw their shadow over him — as he sweetly and humanely says in his pathetic ballad of "The Bridge." One day (after he had bestowed on me the honour and blessing of his friendship, which, thank God, I never lost) he chanced to stop his carriage just in front of the old Tudor Building, in Court Street, Boston, to speak to me; and I remember observing then the sweet, wistful, half-sad, far-away look in his sensitive face, and thinking he looked like a man who had suffered, or might yet suffer, great affliction. There was a strange touch of sorrowful majesty and prophetic fortitude commingled with the composure and kindness of his features.

It was in April, 1854, that I became personally acquainted with Longfellow, and he was the first literary friend I ever had — greeting me as a young aspirant in literature, and holding out to me the hand of fellowship and encouragement. He allowed me to dedicate to him a volume of my verses, published in that year, being the first of my ventures. They were juvenile and crude verses; yet he was tolerant of them, because he knew the sincerity of heart and ambition of spirit that lay beneath them, and, in his far-reaching charity and prescience, he must have thought that something good might come, even of such a poor beginning. At all events, where others were cold, or satirical, or contemptuous, he was kind, cordial, and full of cheer. A few words in lenient commendation of the book had been written by N. P. Willis, and the paragraph happened to come in his way. He was pleased with it, and I can hear now the hearty tone in which he spoke of it, turning to Mrs. Longfellow, who was present, and saying, with an obvious relish of good-will: "There is much kindness in Willis's nature." This was a little trait, but it is of little traits that the greatest human character is composed. Goodness, generosity, and a large liberality of judgment were, in his character, conspicuous elements. His spontaneous desire — the natural instinct of his great heart and massive, philosophic mind — was to be helpful: to lift up the lowly; to strengthen the weak; to bring out the best in every person; to dry every tear, and make every pathway smooth. It is saying but little to say that he never spoke a harsh word, except against injustice and wrong. He was the natural friend and earnest advocate of every good cause and right idea. His words about the absent were always considerate, and he never lost a practical opportunity of doing good.

For the infirmities of humanity he was charity itself, and he shrank from harshness as from a positive sin. "It is the prerogative of the poet," he once said to me, in those old days, "to give pleasure; but it is the critic's province to give pain." He had, indeed, but a slender esteem for the critic's province. Yet his tolerant nature found excuses for even as virulent and hostile a critic as his assailant and traducer Edgar Allan Poe — of whom I have heard him speak with genuine pity. His words were few and unobtrusive, and they clearly indicated his consciousness that Poe had grossly abused and maligned him; but instead of resentment for injury they displayed only sorrow for an unfortunate and half-crazed adversary. There was a little volume of Poe's poems — an English edition — on the library table, and at sight of this I was prompted to ask Longfellow if Poe had ever personally met him — "because," I said, "if he had known you, it is impossible he could have written about you in such a manner." He answered that he had never seen Poe, and that the bitterness was, doubtless, due to a deplorable literary jealousy. Then, after a pause of musing, he added, very gravely: "My works seemed to give him much trouble, first and last; but Mr. Poe is dead and gone, and I am alive and still writing — and that is the end of the matter. I never condescended to answer Mr. Poe's attacks; and I would advise you now, at the outset of your literary life, never to take notice of any attacks that may be made upon you. Let them all pass." He then took up the volume of Poe, and, turning the leaves, particularly commended the stanzas entitled "For Annie" and "The Haunted Palace." Then, still speaking of criticism, he mentioned the great number of newspaper and magazine articles, about his own writings, that were received by him — sent, apparently, by their writers. "I look at the first few lines," he said, "and if I find that the article has been written in a pleasant spirit, I read it through; but if I find that the intention is to wound, I drop the paper into my fire, and so dismiss it. In that way one escapes much annoyance."

Longfellow liked to talk of young poets, and he

had an equally humorous and kind way of noticing the foibles of the literary character. Standing in the porch, one summer day, and observing the noble elms in front of his house, he recalled a visit made to him, long before, by one of the many bards, now extinct, who are embalmed in Griswold. Then suddenly assuming a burly, martial air, he seemed to reproduce for me the exact figure and manner of the youthful enthusiast — who had tossed back his long hair, gazed approvingly on the elms, and in a deep voice exclaimed, "I see, Mr. Longfellow, that you have many trees — I love trees!!" "It was," said the poet, "as if he gave a certificate to all the neighbouring vegetation." A few words like these, said in Longfellow's peculiar, dry, humorous manner, with a twinkle of the eye and a quietly droll inflection of the voice, had a certain charm of mirth that cannot be described. It was that same demure playfulness which led him, when writing, to speak of the lady who wore flowers "on the congregation side of her bonnet," or to extol those broad, magnificent western roads, which "dwindle to a squirrel-track, and run up a tree." He had no particle of the acidity of sparkling and biting wit; but he had abundant, playful humour, that was full of kindness, and that toyed good-naturedly with all the trifles of life. That such a sense of fun should be amused by the ludicrous peculiarities of a juvenile bard was inevitable.

I recall many talks with him, about poetry and

the avenues of literary labour, and the discipline of the mind in youth. His counsel was always summed up in two words — calmness and patience. He did not believe in seeking experience, or in going to meet burdens. "What you desire will come, if you will but wait for it" — that he said to me again and again. "My ambition once was," he remarked, "to edit a magazine. Since then the opportunity has been offered to me many times — and I did not take it, and would not." That same night he spoke of his first poem — the first that ever was printed — and described his trepidation, when going, in the evening, to drop the precious manuscript into the editor's box. This was at a newspaper office in Portland, Maine, when he was a boy. Publication day arrived and the paper came out — but not a word of the poem. "But I had another copy," he said, "and I immediately sent it to the rival paper, and it was published." And then he described his exultation and inexpressible joy and pride, when, — having bought a copy of the paper, still damp from the press, and walked with it into a by-street of the town, — he saw, for the first time, a poem of his own actually in print! "I have never since had such a thrill of delight," he said, "over any of my publications."

His sense of humour found especial pleasure in the inappropriate words that were sometimes said to him by persons whose design it was to be complimentary, and he would relate, with a keen relish of their pleasantry, anecdotes, to illustrate this form of social blunder. Years ago he told me, at Cambridge, about the strange gentleman who was led up to him and introduced, at Newport, and who straightway said, with enthusiastic fervour, — "Mr. Longfellow, I have long desired the honour of knowing you! Sir, I am one of *the few* men who have read your 'Evangeline.'" Another of his favourites was related to me a day or two after it occurred. The poet's rule was to reserve the morning for work, and visitors were not received before 12 o'clock, noon. One morning a man forced his way past the servant who had opened the hall-door, and bursting upon the presence of the astonished author, in his library, addressed him in the following remarkable words: "Mr. Longfellow, you're a poet, I believe, and so I've called here to see if I couldn't git you to write some poetry, for me to have printed, and stuck onto my medicine bottles. You see, I go round sellin' this medicine, and if you give me the poetry, I'll give you a bottle of the carminative — and it's one dollar a bottle." For the full enjoyment of this story it was needful to see the poet's face and hear the bland tone of his voice. More than twenty-four years ago he told me that incident — sitting by the wide fire-place, in the library back of his study. As I write his words now, the wind seems again to be moaning in the chimney, and the fire-light flickers upon his pale, handsome, happy face, and already silvered hair. He took delight in any bit of quiet fun, like that. He was always gracious, always kind, always wishful to make every one happy that came near him!

About poetry he talked with the earnestness of what was a genuine passion, and yet with no particle of self-assertion. Tennyson's "Princess" was a new book when first I heard him speak of it, and I remember Mrs. Longfellow sitting with that volume in her hands and reading it by the evening lamp. The delicate loveliness of the little lyrical pieces that are interspersed throughout its text was, in particular, dwelt upon as a supreme merit. Among his own poems his favourite at that time was "Evangeline"; but he said that the style of versification which pleased him best was that of "The Day is Done"; nor do I wonder, reading this now, together with "The Bridge," "Twilight," "The Children's Hour," and "The Open Window," and finding them so exquisite both in pathos and music. He said also that he sometimes wrote poems that were for himself alone, that he should not care ever to publish, because they were too delicate for publication. One of his sayings was that "the desire of the young poet is not for applause, but for recognition." He much commended the example, in one respect, of the renowned Italian poet Alfieri, who caused himself to be bound into his library chair and left for a certain period of time, each day, at his library table — his servants being strictly enjoined not to release him till that time had passed: by this means he forced himself to labour. No man ever believed more firmly than Longfellow did in regular, proportioned, resolute, incessant industry. His poem of "The Builders" contains his creed; his poem of "The Ladder of St. Augustine" is the philosophy of his career. Yet I have many times heard him say "the mind cannot be controlled"; and the fact that he was, when at his best, a poet of pure inspiration is proved, beyond possibility of doubt, by such poems as "Sandalphon," "My Lost Youth," "The Beleaguered City," "The Fire of Drift Wood," "Suspiria," "The Secret of the Sea," "The Two Angels," and "The Warden of the Cinque Ports." Either of them is worthy of the brightest name that ever was written on the scroll of the lyric muse.

The two writers of whom he oftenest spoke, within my hearing, were Lowell and Hawthorne. Of Lowell he said, "He is one of the manliest and noblest men that ever lived." "Hawthorne often came into this room," he said, "and sometimes he would go there, behind the window curtains, and remain in silent reverie the whole evening. No one disturbed him; he came and went as he liked. He was a mysterious man." With Irving's works he was especially familiar, and he often quoted from them, in his talk to me. One summer day at his cottage at Nahant I found him reading Cooper's sea stories, and had the comfort of hearing from his lips a tribute to that great writer — the foremost novelist in American literature, unmatched since Scott, in the power to treat with a free inspiration and vigorous and splendid descriptive skill the vast pageants of nature, and to build and sustain ideals of human character worthy of such surroundings. Longfellow was in fine spirits that day, and very happy, and I have always thought of him as he looked then, holding his daughter Edith in his arms — a little child, with long, golden hair, and lovely, merry face — and, by his mere presence, making the sunshine brighter and the place more sacred with kindness and peace.

The best portrait of Longfellow is the one made by Samuel Lawrence; and it is the best because it gives the noble and spirited poise and action of his head, shows his clean-cut, strong, yet delicate features unmasked with a beard, and preserves that alert, inspired expression which came into his face when he was affected by any strong emotion. I recall Mrs. Longfellow's commendation of it, in a fireside talk. It was her favourite portrait of him. We discussed together Thomas Buchanan Read's portrait of him, and of his three daughters, when those pictures were yet fresh from the easel. I remember speaking to him of a fancied resemblance between the face of Mrs. Longfellow and the face of "Evangeline," in Faed's well-known picture. He said that others had noticed it, but

that he himself did not perceive it. Yet I think
those faces were alike, in stateliness and in the
mournful beauty of the eyes. It is strange what
trifles crowd upon the memory, when one thinks
of the long ago and the friends that have departed.
I recollect his smile when he said that he always
called to mind the number of the house in Beacon
Street, Boston, — which was Mrs. Longfellow's
home when she was Miss Appleton, — "by think-
ing of the 39 Articles." I recollect the gentle
gravity of his voice when he showed me a piece of
the coffin of Dante, and said, in a low tone, "That
has touched his bones." I recollect the benignant
look in his eyes and the warm pressure of his hand
when he bade me good-bye (it was the last time),
saying, "You never forget me — you always come
to see me." There were long lapses of time during
which I never saw him, being held fast by incessant
duties and driven far away, by the gales of life,
from the old moorings of my youth. But, as often
as I came back to his door, his love met me on
the threshold, and his noble serenity gave me com-
fort and peace. It is but a little while ago since,
in quick and delicate remembrance of the old days,
he led me to his hearthstone, saying, "Come and
sit in my children's chair." What an awful solem-
nity, and yet what a soothing sense of perfect
nobleness and beneficent love, must hallow now
that storied home from which his earthly and visi-
ble presence has forever departed!

Twenty years ago last summer, on a day of sunshine and flowers and gently whispering winds, those rooms were hushed and darkened, and a group of mourning friends stood around the sacred relics — beautiful in death — of the poet's wife. Only one voice was heard — the voice of prayer. But every heart prayed for the lonely sufferer, thus awfully stricken and left to bear the burden of a great and endless grief. And then we followed her to the place of her final rest. Here before me is a twig that I broke, that day, from a tree beside her grave. I may keep it now in remembrance of him as well as of her. He has fulfilled within twenty years some of the greatest works of his life; but in all that time he has only been waiting for the hour which came to him at last. Through all the grand poise of his being, through his never-ending still beginning labour, through his quiet ways neither mournful nor gay, through his meek but manly acceptance of all the events of life, through the high and solemn strains of his latter poetry, and through that wistful, haunted look in his venerable, bard-like countenance, this was the one prevailing truth. He was waiting for the end. We who loved him must mourn for him, but not in despairing gloom. The world is lonelier for his absence. "Woe is me, that I should gaze upon thy place and find it vacant!"

> "O friend! O best of friends! Thy absence more
> Than the impending night darkens the landscape o'er!"

Yet let us think of the great life that he so amply and nobly filled and accomplished; his grand conquest of trouble; the vast treasure of wisdom and beauty that he has left in the world to comfort and strengthen and guide us; the relief that he has found from sadness, sickness, and age; the happiness into which assuredly he has entered! Let us turn to his own words, and take comfort once more from that loving heart which was always so ready to give it: "Death is neither an end nor a beginning. It is a transition, not from one existence to another, but from one state of existence to another. No link is broken in the chain of being; any more than in passing from infancy to manhood, from manhood to old age. . . . Death brings us again to our friends. They are waiting for us, and we shall not long delay. They have gone before us, and are like the angels in heaven. They stand upon the borders of the grave to welcome us, with the countenance of affection which they wore on earth; yet more lovely, more radiant, more spiritual. . . . The far country toward which we journey seems nearer to us, and the way less dark; for thou hast gone before, passing so quietly to thy rest that day itself dies not more calmly."

> "O though oft depressed and lonely,
>   All my fears are laid aside,
> If I but remember only
>   Such as these have lived and died."

III.

ELEGY ON THE DEATH OF LONGFELLOW.

(Obiit March 24th, 1882.)

ALONE, at night, he heard them sigh —
  These wild March winds that beat his tomb —
Alone, at night, from those that die,
  He sought one ray, to light his gloom.

And still he heard the night winds moan,
  And still the mystery closed him round,
And still the darkness, cold and lone,
  Sent forth no ray, returned no sound.

But Time at last the answer brings,
    And he, past all our suns and snows,
At rest with peasants and with kings,
    Like them the wondrous secret knows.

Alone, at night, we hear them sigh —
    These wild March winds that stir his pall;
And, helpless, wandering, lost, we cry
    To his dim ghost, to tell us all.

He loved us, while he lingered here;
    We loved him — never love more true!
He will not leave, in doubt and fear,
    The human grief that once he knew.

For never yet was born the day,
    When, faint of heart and weak of limb,
One suffering creature turned away,
    Unhelped, unsoothed, uncheered by him!

But still through darkness, dense and bleak,
    The winds of March moan wildly round,
And still we feel that all we seek
    Ends in that sigh of vacant sound.

He cannot tell us — none can tell
    What waits behind the mystic veil!
Yet he who lived and died so well,
    In that, perchance, has told the tale.

Not to the wastes of Nature drift —
    Else were this world an evil dream —
The crown and soul of Nature's gift,
    By Avon or by Charles's stream.

His heart was pure, his purpose high,
    His thought serene, his patience vast;
He put all strifes of passion by,
    And lived to God, from first to last.

His song was like the pine-tree's sigh,
    At midnight o'er a poet's grave,
Or like the sea-bird's distant cry,
    Borne far across the twilight wave.

There is no flower of meek delight,
    There is no star of heavenly pride,
That shines not fairer and more bright
    Because he lived, loved, sang, and died.

Wild winds of March, his requiem sing!
    Weep o'er him, April's sorrowing skies!
Till come the tender flowers of Spring
    To deck the pillow where he lies:

Till violets pour their purple flood,
    That wandering myrtle shall not lack,
And, royal with the summer's blood,
    The roses that he loved come back:

Till all that Nature gives of light,
    To rift the gloom and point the way,
Shall sweetly pierce our mortal night,
    And symbol his immortal day!

WANDERERS.

THE WRECKER'S BELL.

A Ballad.

I.

THERE'S a lurid light in the clouds to-night,
   In the wind there's a desolate moan;
And the rage of the furious sea is white,
   Where it beats on the crags of stone:
Stand here at my side, and look over the tide,
   And say if you hear it, — the sullen knell,
Faint, from afar, on the harbor-bar,
   The hollow boom of the wrecker's bell.
For I cannot hear — I am cold with fear —
   Ah, leave me not alone!
For I'm old, I'm old, and my blood is cold,
   And I fear to be alone.

II.

With a shudder I saw his ashen face,
  In that wild and fearful night —
For his blazing eyes illumed the place
  With a terrible, ghastly light;
And ever his long locks floated out,
  As white as the foam of the sea;
And the great waves dashed on the rocks about
  With a mad and cruel glee.
But I stood by his side, and looked over the tide,
  And faintly I heard that solemn knell,
Faint, from afar, on the harbor-bar,
  The hollow boom of the wrecker's bell.

III.

It is but the clang of the signal bell,
  That floats through the midnight air:
For many a year, in the surging swell,
  Has the old bell sounded there.
When the storm in his might rides through the night
  And his steeds in thunder neigh,
Then its iron tongue is swayed and swung,
  And plunged in the angry spray;

And so when the summer skies are bright,
   And the breakers are at play.
But wherefore is it you stay me here,
   And why do you shudder and moan,
And what are the nameless shapes you fear
   In this desolate place alone?
For your eyes are set in a dreadful glare,
   And you shrink at the solemn knell,
As it trembles along the midnight air —
   The boom of the wrecker's bell.

IV.

Look up, he cried, to the awful sky,
   Look over the furious sea,
And mark, as the grinning fiends float by,
   How they beckon and howl to me!
They are ringing my knell with the baleful bell,
   And they gloat on the doom to be.
Ah! give me your hand, and look not back —
   We stand not here alone —
And the horrible shapes that throng my track
   Would turn your heart to stone.
The spell of the dead is on the hour,
And I yield my soul to its fearful power.

V.

A face looks forth in the darkness there,
    A young face, sweet with a rosy light:
The sunshine sleeps in her golden hair,
    And her violet eyes are softly bright:
On her parted lips there's an innocent smile,
    Like a sunbeam kissing a velvet rose;
And her cheeks of pearl grow warm the while,
    With a delicate blush that comes and goes.
Ah! purer than morn in its purest hour,
    And holy as one from an angel clime,
Was the tender woman, the beautiful flower,
    I loved and lost in the far-off time.

VI.

One fatal night, in the long ago,
    My gallant cruiser passed that bar.
In a bank of clouds the moon hung low,
    And the sombre sky showed never a star.
The night was calm, but I heard in the swell
    A murmur of storm, and, far away,
The muffled toll of the wrecker's bell,
    As it floated up from the outer bay.

And a look of hate in the waiting waves
Spoke to my soul of a place of graves.

VII.

I watched them there, as I stood at the wheel, —
The happy lover, the radiant bride, —
And the wasting fever of frantic pain
And terrible passion burnt my brain;
And I felt what only demons feel,
For the man who walked by that woman's side.
With gentle murmur the lovers talked,
As to and fro on the deck they walked.
Nothing they thought of danger then,
Or the schemes and crimes of wicked men.
Wrapt in a quiet dream of bliss,
And consecrate with a marriage kiss,
What could those innocent creatures know
Of the burning hate and the maddening woe,
And the deadly purpose of blind despair,
In the heart of the fiend beside them there!

VIII.

An hour had passed — he stood alone, —
  I thought no creature saw the blow

That felled him, senseless as a stone,
Or heard the pitiful, low moan,
  His death-sigh, as he sank below
  These very waters where they flow
    Around that vengeful bell.
But joy, like grief, will vigils keep;
And love hath eyes that never sleep,
    And secret tongues that tell.
She passed me like a bolt of light,
A heavenly angel robed in white!
One dazzling gleam, one cry so shrill
That sea and sky and this lone hill
Are echoing with its anguish still —
And she had leaped into the night:
And on her murdered lover's breast
In the same wave she sunk to rest.
  That moment o'er the sky
Flamed the red wrath of such a storm
As might enwreathe the Avenger's form,
  When howling fiends defy.
No ship could live in the gale that blew,
And mine went down with all her crew —
  I only left alive!
Spurned upward out of weltering hell

To that same reef where swings the bell
That, ever since, with fateful spell,
Hath drawn me by its hideous knell,
 I breathed, and ceased to strive —
I, whom the lightning will not rend,
Nor waves engulf, nor death befriend,
 Nor holy father shrive! . . .

IX.

There's a lurid light in the clouds to-night,
 In the wind there's a desolate moan;
But the waves roll soft on the sand so white,
 And break on the crags of stone;
And the sea-gulls scream in their frolic flight,
 And all my dream is flown.
But, far away in the twilight gloom,
I still can hear it, the muffled boom, —
And it seems to be ringing a dead man's knell, —
Solemn and slow, of the wrecker's bell.

ACCOMPLICES.

[The Murderer.]

Black rocks upon the dreadful coast,
    Mutter no more my hidden crime!
I hear, far off, your sullen boast,
    But I defy you! 't is not time!

You cannot tell our secret yet;
    The trusty sea must keep its dead,
And many suns arise and set
    Before that awful word is said.

I am but young; I 've all the grace
    Of life, and love, and beauty now:
There 's not a wrinkle on my face;
    There 's not a shadow on my brow.

Accomplices.

I cannot bear the darksome grave
    I will not leave the cheerful sun!
Rave on! in storm and midnight rave,
    For years and years, till all is done.

Till these brown locks are changed to gray;
    Till these clear eyes are dim and old;
Not yet, not yet the fatal day
    When all that horror must be told!

But, then — gnash all your jagged teeth,
    And howl for vengeance! I will come;
And that same cruel pit beneath
    Shall yawn and gulf me to my home.

To-day — forbear, nor mutter more!
    The sky is dark, and dark the sea,
And all the land from shore to shore
    Is hideous with your grisly glee.

A DREAM OF THE PAST.

I.

THE peace of this autumnal day
   Allures my dreaming thoughts away,
To that great world beyond the deep
Where I so many treasures keep.
There, fond and true, one friend I find,
Whose tender heart and constant mind
Gave, while he lingered here on earth,
Comfort, and cheer, and hope, and mirth;
And still they waft a cordial breath
Across the icy waves of death.
His nature, while he dwelt below,
Was like these days: this season's glow,
The misty sky, the sleeping sea,
The browning grass, the burnished tree,

The wild flowers, swinging o'er the brook,
Were in his heart as in his book.
Alive, he charmed away life's fret
With all the sunshine he could get,
And, when death whispered, softly crept
Into a quiet place and slept;
And Nature never saw such grace
As hallowed then his noble face.
And so, to think upon him here,
In this sweet season of the year, —
Which he so loved, which he was like
As clouds are to the clouds they strike, —
Is winning peace, and strength to live,
Beyond what all the world can give.

II.

Ah, not to me, dear heart, was said
The word that crowned thy royal head
First with the aureole's light and bloom,
And then the amaranth of the tomb.
Fate gave thee power, and calm, and poise,
And all thy days and deeds were joys.
Thine were the forest and the flood,
The sunrise sparkled in thy blood,

And thou didst hold a careless flight
Above the dells and caves of night.
But ever through thy smile shone clear
The lustre of compassion's tear,
The pity of thy gentle mind,
And tenderness, for all mankind.
I saw thee with a wistful eye,
And saddened — and I knew not why;
Till soon, too soon, thy summons came,
And thou wert nothing but a name.
Ah, day of misery and of moan,
When grief and I were left alone!

III.

Fate gave not me her smile benign —
That pensive, playful calm of thine —
But early from her bosom cast,
To be the sport of every blast,
To war with passion, and to know
The sting of want, the pang of woe, —
Forcing a soul, for kindness born,
To every strife it held in scorn.
So, careless whether right or wrong,
I battled through the hostile throng,

And felt, whatever doom might be,
Or life or death the same to me.
'T was then across my pathway lone
The holy star of friendship shone !
'T was then thy kindness soothed my pain,
And arched the heaven of hope again !
As, sudden through the stormy dark,
Full on the tempest-battered barque,
Home's glad and golden beacons shine,
So flashed thy spirit upon mine :
And not, though Hope's last star were set,
Could this true heart of mine forget !

IV.

Now, of our few but happy years
Remains this flower, that bloomed in tears:
   Not of the crown of life bereft
   Is he who yet has patience left.
The haggard sky, the surf's dull roar,
The midnight storm, are mine no more :
But mine the gleam of setting sun,
The call of birds when day is done,
The last, sad light, so loath to pass
   weeps upon the golden grass,

The sigh of leaves in evening air,
The distant bell that calls to prayer, —
And nothing from my spirit bars
The benediction of the stars.

v.

Ah, loved so well and mourned so long,
Here in my heart as in my song,
To thy dear memory let me raise
One tender strain of other days,
One pæan to the good thou wast,
One low lament for all I lost.
Yet, looking o'er life's arid track,
Kind soul, I would not wish thee back.
What sadder lot, what doom of fate,
More sterile is, more desolate,
Than here to goad our wearied powers,
And toil through times that are not ours!
Ah, no, the silence now is best,
The leaf down-fluttering o'er thy rest,
And every kind, caressing sigh
That Nature breathes o'er those that die:
While thou, in some serener sphere,
Forget'st the toils and troubles here;

Or, made a part of flowers and trees,
Art pure, and calm, and safe, like these.
— Slow pales the light; the day declines;
The night-wind murmurs in the pines;
The stars come out, and, far away,
Across the sweetly sleeping bay
One snow-white sail, by sunset kist,
Fades slowly in the ocean mist,
Fades — like all joys and griefs we know,
And like this dream of Long Ago.

OCTOBER, 1881.

HOMEWARD BOUND.

I.

ON roseate shores, in evening's glow,
    With pulsing music soft and sweet,
While winds of summer gently blow,
    The waves of Time's great ocean beat;
No cloud obscures the heavenly dome,
    And only on the shining sea
The tossing crests of silver foam
    Presage the tempest yet to be.

II.

Low down upon the ocean's verge,
    Blent with the waters and the skies,
Far, far across the sounding surge,
    The Golden City's towers arise :

Fair in the sunset light they gleam,
   Youth's chosen realm, bold manhood's goal,
The promised land of fancy's dream,
   The Golden City of the soul!

III.

How softly bright, how purely cold,
   Those domes and pinnacles of bliss!
How radiant, through its gates of gold,
   That world of rapture smiles on this!
How glorious, in the dying day,
   O'er bastion ridge and glimmering moat,
Through rainbow clouds and rosy spray,
   Its purple banners flash and float!

IV.

There, safe from every mortal ill,
   Waits every wasted love of man;
The hopes that Time could ne'er fulfil,
   And only Death and Nature can!
There peace shall touch the eyes of grief,
   And mercy soothe the heart of pain;
And every bud, and flower, and leaf
   That withered here shall bloom again!

V.

Ah, sailor to the golden realm,
  With hope's glad haven just before,
Why muse beside the idle helm,
  With listless glances back to shore?
Night hovers o'er his trackless way,
  To blot the stars and dim the land;
What voice is at his heart, to stay
  The signal wafture of his hand?

VI.

Not thus, in other days, his soul
  Of power and trust could wander back —
But saw the mists of time unroll,
  And angels throng his shining track;
Heard mystic voices, from afar,
  Of warders on the sacred coast;
Sprang up to meet the morning star
  And mingle with the heavenly host.

VII.

But he has borne the rage of storms,
  Through many a slow and patient year,

Still following those celestial forms
    That beckon and elude him here:
Till doubt has dimmed his eager gaze,
    And toil subdued his ardent mind,
And sorrow burdened all his days
    With quest of peace he shall not find.

VIII.

Her kiss is cold upon his lips,
    Who swore to be forever true;
His eyes have seen youth's phantom ships
    Fade down beyond the distant blue;
His hand has cleared the gathering moss
    From many a tablet, cold and white,
Where, dark with sense of doom and loss,
    His comrades sleep, in starless night.

IX.

The wayward shafts of cruel fate,
    That strike the best and purest lives;
The curse of blessings come too late;
    The broken faith that life survives;

Love's frail pretence, ambition's lure,
    Malignant envy's poisoned dart,
That wounds and tortures, past all cure,
    The mangled, seared, imbittered heart;—

X.

The weary, wistful, sad repose
    Of ardour quenched and feeling sped;
The arid calm he only knows
    Whose hope is — like his idols — dead;
All that repentant spirits bear,
    For sin and folly past recall;
Remorse, endurance, patience, care —
    His soul has known and borne them all.

XI.

Ah, touch him gently, winds of night,
    And ocean odours, vague and strange,
Revive his morn of young delight —
    Supreme o'er doubt, and fear, and change!
The fading tints of life restore,
    The wasted fires of youth relume —
And round his radiant path once more
    Let music sound and roses bloom!

XII.

Long has he gazed in Nature's eyes,
   Long kept the faith her glory yields
The pageants of the starry skies,
   The flowery pomp of spangled fields,
The fragrant depth of woodland ways,
   White in the moon, or dusk and dim,
And lonely mountain tops that blaze
   Through sunset lustre, vast and grim.

XIII.

Long has he bowed at Nature's shrine —
   Shall Nature's soul desert him now?
Ah, shine again, thou star divine,
   And touch with light his darkening brow!
Though pleasures pall, though idols fall,
   Though wisdom end in long regret,
Death's glorious conquest pays for all,
   And He who made will not forget! . .

XIV.

The day is done, the storm is free,
   And night and danger ride the gale;

But, bravely speeding, far at sea,
   Gleams, white and clear, one lessening sail!
One moment seen, now lost to sight,
   'Mid driving cloud and ocean's roar;
But, steered by God's own beacon light,
   He yet shall reach the golden shore.

THE POET'S LIFE.

I.

ORDAINED to work the heavenly will
  Comes a bright angel, sent from far;
And Nature feels another thrill,
  And Love has lit another star.

II.

Earth was more beautiful because of him.
    Wild flowers were born;
  And limpid, bickering brooks,
  The poet's earliest books,
  Spoke of a new delight
    Unto the morn:
  And, in the fragrant night,
When fairies, sporting underneath the moon,
    In airy glee
    And revelry,

Made the wide darkness beautifully bright,
Like brightest noonday in the heart of June,
   Every wavelet laughed, and after
   Seemed to chase its nimble laughter;
     Till spent,
    With emulous merriment,
It sunk to sleep in some secluded, cool,
   And black and lucent pool.

III.

   On meadows starred with daisies
   The wild bee swooned, in mazes
   Of witching odour, richer far
   Than spikenard, rose, and jasmine are.
All natural objects seemed to catch a rare and
     precious gleam.
   Unknowing why, the happy birds
   Trilled out their hearts in seeming joyous words,
   All indistinct, though sweet, to mortal ears;
   Such as a poet hears,
   With joy and yet with tears,
In some ethereal reverie, half vision and half dream.

Through breezy tree-tops jocund voices thrilled,
    And, deep in slumberous caverns of the ocean,
    Wild Echo heard, and with an airy motion
Tossed back the greeting of a heart o'er-filled
With gladness, and that speaks it o'er and o'er,
    Till bliss can say no more.
The waves that whispered on the listening sands
Told the glad tidings unto many lands,
And the stars heard, and from their wandering isles
Dropt down the blessing of their golden smiles. . . .

IV.

Touched by the lightning of the Maker's eyes
    He spake in prophecies,
Interpreting the earth, the sea, the skies —
    All that in Nature is of mystery,
      All that in Man is dark,
    All that the perfect future is to be,
      When quenched our mortal spark
    And souls imprisoned are at last set free.
Backward he gazed, across the eternal sea,
    And on the ever-lessening shores of time
    Saw ghosts of ruined empires wandering slow.

Then, onward looking, saw the radiant bow
Of promise, shining o'er a heavenly clime.
And thus he knew of life its mystic truth —
Hope, with perpetual youth,
And that wherein all doubt and trouble cease,
Sweet child of patience, peace.

V.

And now came death, a gentle, welcome guest,
And touched his hand and led him into rest.
Time paid its tribute to eternity —
A great soul, ripe for the immortal day —
And earth embraced his ashes : cold their bed,
For now the aged year was also dead.
The winter wind shrieked loud, with hoarse alarms,
  The keen stars shivered in the midnight air,
And the bare trees stretched forth their stiffened arms
  To the wan sky, in pale and speechless prayer.

VI.

Speak softly here, and softly tread,
  For all the place is holy ground

Where Nature's love enshrines her dead,
   And earth with blessing folds them round.

He rests at last: the world far-off
   May riot in her mad excess,
But now her plaudit and her scoff,
   To him alike are nothingness.

He learned in depths where virtue fell
   The heights to which the soul may rise:
He sounded the abyss of hell,
   He scaled the walls of paradise.

What else? Till every wandering star
   In heaven's blue vault be cold and dim,
Our faithful spirits, following far,
   Walk in the light that falls from him.

THE MERRY MONARCH.

I.

IT comes into my mind, in a genial mood,
    When the worlds of my being, without and within,
Are quietly happy, in all that is good,
    Unclouded by care and untempted by sin, —
If the gods would but grant me my dearest desire,
    As I fancy, sometimes, they 're inclining to do,
That I should n't sit here, looking into the fire,
    And dreaming, my love, as I 'm dreaming of you.

II.

Nor should I be thinking, as sometimes I am, —
    If the gods had but made me the thing I would be, —
That a station of rank, in a world full of sham,
    Were a pleasant and suitable station for me.

Nor should I be striving, with heart and with brain,
    For the laurel that poets are anxious to wear, —
That dubious guerdon for labour and pain,
    That sorry exchange for the natural hair.

III.

No ! I never should care, if I had my own way,
    For the storm or the sunshine, the Yes or the No ;
But, quietly careless and perfectly gay,
    I could let the world go as it wanted to go.
I should ask neither riches, nor station, nor power ;
    They are chances, they happen, and there is an end ;
But a heart that beats merrily every hour
    Is a god's richest gift, is a man's truest friend.

IV.

And that's what I'd have ! For that blessing I pray !
    A spirit so gentle and easy and bright,
It would gladden with sunshine the sunniest day,
    And with magical splendour illumine the night.
I could envy no potentate under the sun,
    However sublime might that potentate be ;
For I'd live, the illustrious Monarch of Fun,
    And the rest of the world should be happy with me.

V.

I 'd be gold in the sunshine and silver in showers;
    I 'd be rainbows, and clouds all of purple and pearl;
And the fairies of fun should laugh out of the flowers,
    And the jolly old earth should be all in a whirl!
The brooks should trill music, the leaves dance in glee,
    And old ocean should bellow with surly delight:
O, but would n't it be something festal to see,
    If the gods did but grant me my kingdom to-night!

VI.

And I think it will come, — that succession of mine
    That crown with the opals of jollity set;
And the joy in my soul will be something divine
    When I finally teach myself how to forget;
Forget every sorrow in which I 've a part,
    All the dreams that allure and the hopes that betray;
Contented to wait, with a right merry heart,
    For silence and night and the end of the play.

BLUE EYES AND BLACK.

A Song.

I.

HERE'S a health to the lass with the merry
    black eyes!
Here's a health to the lad with the blue ones!
Here's a bumper to love, as it sparkles and flies,
    And here's joy to the hearts that are true ones!
Yes, joy to the hearts that are tender and true, —
    With a passion that nothing can smother!
To the eyes of the one, that are pensive and blue,
    And the merry black eyes of the other!

II.

Mind this now, my lad, with the sweet eyes of blue,
    That, whatever the graces invite you,
There is nothing for you in this world that will do
    But a pair of black eyes to delight you:

And mind, my gay lass, with the dear eyes of black,
    In a pair of blue eyes to discover
That pure light of affection you never should lack, —
    And you 'll always be true to your lover!

III.

Long, long shall your eyes sparkle back with a kiss
    To the eyes that live but to behold you:
Long, long shall the magic of mutual bliss
    In a heaven of rapture enfold you!
And forever to you shall that singer[1] be wise,
    Whose sweet thought is the truest of true ones, —
That the answering lustre of merry black eyes
    Is the life of a pair of true blue ones.

[1] Goethe, *in* "*Wilhelm Meister.*" — "*To look on a pair of bright black eyes is the life of a pair of blue ones.*"

OLD TIMES.

ROSY days of youth and fancy,
    Happy hours of long ago!
Ah, the flickering sunbeam visions —
    How they waver to and fro!

Galaxies of blue-eyed Marys,
    With a Julia and a Jane,
And a troop of little Lauras,
    Blush, and laugh, and romp again.

Moonlight meetings, dreamy rambles,
    In the balm of summer night,
When our hearts were full of rapture
    And our senses of delight, —

These remember — and remember
   How the fond stars shone above,
Keeping in their mellow splendour
   Watch and ward upon our love.

Youth is like the diamond dawning —
   Bold it breaks to gorgeous day;
Heavenly fires of power and beauty
   Blaze and burn along its way.

Far within its mystic future
   Oft are solemn voices heard!
Shaped to many a stately anthem
   Floats the music of a word.

But that music, in the present,
   Droops with passion's dull decay,
Till its echo, in the spirit,
   Faints, and fails, and dies away.

Green be then the tender memory
   Of the past, forever sped,
So that youth may be immortal,
   Though its days and dreams are dead!

JOHN McCULLOUGH.

Read at a Banquet at Delmonico's, New York, April 4, 1881.

LONG hushed is the harp that his glory had spoken,
  Long stilled is the heart that could summon its strain;
Now its chords are all silent, or tuneless, or broken,
  What touch can awaken its music again!

Ah, the breeze in the green dells of Erin is blowing!
  If not her great bard yet her spirit can flame,
When proud where the waters of Shannon are flowing
  Her groves and her temples re-echo his name.

Float softly o'er shamrocks, and blue-bells, and roses,
   Blend all their gay tints and their odours in one;
And sweet as the zephyr in twilight that closes
   Be the kiss of thy love on the brows of thy son!

Breathe tenderly o'er us, who cluster around him,
   In this, his glad moment of triumph and pride:
Deep, deep in our souls are the ties that have bound
     him,
   And life will be lone, with his presence denied.

From the arms of the mother, in childhood a rover,
   To exile he came, on the wanderer's shore:
To the arms of the mother, his trials all over,
   And honoured and laurelled, we yield him once
     more.

Speak low of affection that longs to embrace him,
   Speak loud of the fame that awaits him afar —
When homage shall hail him, and beauty shall grace
     him,
   And pomp hang her wreaths on the conqueror's car!

When the shadows of time at his touch fall asunder,
   And heroes and demi-gods leap into light;
When the accents of Brutus ring wild in the thunder,
   And the white locks of Lear toss like sea-foam
      in night;

When the grief of the Moor, like a tempest that dashes
   On crags in mid-ocean, has died into rest;
When the heart of Virginius breaks, o'er the ashes
   Of her who was sweetest, and purest, and best;

How proudly, how gladly their praise will caress him!
   How brightly the jewels will blaze in his crown!
How the white hands of honour will greet him and
      bless him
   With lilies and roses of perfect renown!

Ah, grand is the flight of the eagle of morning,
   While the dark world beneath him drifts into the
      deep;
But cold as the snow-wreaths the mountains adorning
   Is the light that illumines his desolate sweep.

When the trumpets are blown and the standards are streaming,
    And the festal lamps beam on the royal array,
How oft will the heart of the monarch be dreaming
    Of the home and the friends that are far, far away!

There's a pulse in his breast that would always regret us —
    It dances in laughter, it trembles in tears;
With the world at his feet, he would never forget us,
    And our hearts would be true, through an ocean of years!

The cymbals may clash and the gay pennons glisten,
    And the clangour of gladness ring jocund and free,
But, calm in the tumult, his spirit will listen
    For our whisper of love, floating over the sea:

For the music of tones that were once so endearing
    (Like a wind of the west o'er a prairie of flowers),
But that never again will resound in his hearing,
    Except through the tremulous sadness of ours.

Ah, manly and tender, thy deeds are thy praises!
   Speed on in thy grandeur, all peerless and lone,
And greet, in old England, her hawthorns and
      daisies, —
   A spirit as gentle and bright as their own!

Speed on, wheresoever God's angel may guide thee!
   No fancy can dream and no language can tell
What faith and what blessings walk ever beside thee,
   Or the depth of our love as we bid thee Farewell.

LAWRENCE BARRETT.

*Read at a Banquet at the Lotos Club, New York,
June 7, 1881.*

WHEN from his gaze our shores receding
   In night and distance drift away,
And, every present joy unheeding,
   He turns to muse, and grieve, and pray,
How will regret and memory, meeting,
   This brilliant scene bring back to view,
And hear once more your manly greeting,
   And sigh once more his fond adieu!

And we, by sadness made more tender,
   As here we knit our broken chain —
How gladly will affection render
   Our gentle tribute once again!

How sweet 't will be, though joys are thwarted,
   And smiles rebuked by sorrow's sigh,
To think, however friends are parted,
   At least that friendship cannot die!

His eyes will look on English meadows
   Where scarlet poppies smile and dream;
And he will muse where wandering shadows
   Drift over Avon's sacred stream;
And, mind and soul in bondage taken,
   Will roam those temples strange and vast,
Where every pensive step will waken
   The glorious memories of the Past.

But we shall hear, in grief beclouded,
   Poor Harebell mourn his ruined home;
And see, in night and tempest shrouded,
   Grim Cassius pace the stones of Rome;
With grizzled Yorick, frenzy-ridden,
   From passion's fevered dream awake;
And feel, with tears that flow unbidden,
   The royal heart of Scotland break.

O, Art divine, supreme, undying —
   Not Time nor Space can e'er subdue!
The seas roll on — the years are flying —
   Man passes — Thou alone art true!
No cloud can dim their deathless lustre
   Whose names thy angel hands enroll,
Nor blight the shining shapes that cluster
   In thy vast pantheon of the soul!

Yet, many a cherished tie is broken,
   Across that darkening waste of sea! —
They make no sign, they send no token,
   They come not back to love and me.
I know where, deaf to blames and praises,
   In youth and beauty cold and dead,
Rests now beneath old England's daisies
   Her tenderest heart, her loveliest head!

And him we cast the roses after
   Whose cynic smile was humour's kiss —
Whose magic turned the world to laughter —
   Where dwells he, in an hour like this? . . .

Ah, let us think, though gone before us, —
    The vanished friends of days no more, —
They watch with fond affection o'er us,
    And bless us, from their heavenly shore.

I see the radiant phantoms thronging,
    To clasp him in their guardian thrall!
I bless him, by each noble longing
    That e'er his gentle lips let fall!
By all high thought and pure devotion —
    By towering pine and nestling rose!
Farewell, farewell! on land or ocean —
    God bless him, wheresoe'er he goes!

IN HONOUR OF WILLIAM WARREN.

At Boston, October 28, 1882, was commemorated, by appropriate performances, at the Museum, and in other ways, the Fiftieth Anniversary of Mr. Warren's adoption of the profession of the stage. At midnight, after the play, at a supper, in the comedian's home, at No. 2 Bulfinch Place, a Loving Cup was presented to him, — being the gift of Edwin Booth, Joseph Jefferson, Mary Anderson, John McCullough, and Lawrence Barrett, — and, in offering that tribute, the author read this poem : —

RED globes of autumn strew the sod,
    The bannered woods wear crimson shields,
The aster and the golden-rod
    Deck all the fields.

No clarion blast, at morning blown,
    Should greet the way-worn veteran here,
Nor roll of drum nor trumpet-tone
    Assail his ear.

No jewelled ensigns now should smite,
   With jarring flash, down emerald steeps,
Where sweetly in the sunset light
    The valley sleeps.

No bolder ray should bathe this bower
   Than when, above the glimmering stream,
The crescent moon, in twilight's hour,
    First sheds her beam.

No ruder note should break the thrall,
   That love and peace and honour weave,
Than some lone wild-bird's gentle call,
    At summer eve.

But here should float the voice of song —
   Like evening winds in autumn leaves,
Sweet with the balm they waft along
    From golden sheaves.

The sacred Past should feel its spell,
   And here should murmur, soft and low,
The voices that he loved so well, —
    Long, long ago.

The vanished scenes should give to this
    The cherished forms of other days,
And rosy lips, that felt his kiss,
    Breathe out his praise.

The comrades of his young renown
    Should proudly throng around him now,
When falls the spotless laurel crown
    Upon his brow.

Not in their clamorous shouts who make
    The noonday pomp of glory's lord
Does the true soul of manhood take
    Its high reward.

But when from all the glimmering years
    Beneath the moonlight of the past
The strong and tender spirit hears
    " Well done," at last;

When love looks forth from heavenly eyes,
    And heavenly voices make acclaim,
And all his deeds of kindness rise
    To bless his name;

In Honour of William Warren.

When all that has been sweetly blends
   With all that is, and both revere
The life so lovely in its ends,
     So pure, so dear;

Then leaps indeed the golden flame
   Of blissful pride to rapture's brim —
The fire that sacramental fame
     Has lit for him!

For him who, lord of joy and woe,
   Through half a century's snow-white years
Has gently ruled, in humour's glow,
     The fount of tears.

True, simple, earnest, patient, kind,
   Through griefs that many a weaker will
Had stricken dead, his noble mind
     Was constant still.

Sweet, tender, playful, thoughtful, droll,
   His gentle genius still has made
Mirth's perfect sunshine in the soul,
     And Pity's shade.

With amaranths of eternal spring
   Be all his life's calm evening drest,
While summer winds around him sing
     The songs of rest!

And thou, O Memory, strange and dread,
   That stand'st on heaven's ascending slope,
Lay softly on his reverend head
     The wreath of Hope!

So softly, when the port he wins,
   Toward which life's happiest breezes blow,
That where earth ends and heaven begins
     He shall not know.

W. A. S.

[Obiit, January 7, 1883.]

I.

"GOOD Night, my boy;" and with a smile
    He turned his steps and sped away:
Since then 't is but a little while,
    And he is dead to-day:
Dead, and the friend that once I knew,
    My comrade both in joy and pain,
So often tried and always true,
    Will never smile again.

II.

His days were many, and the world
    Had most of all his thought and care;
But now his sails of toil were furled
    In Art's serener air.

The evening lamp, the storied page,
    The mantling glass, the song, the jest —
These turned the twilight of his age
    To morning and to rest.

III.

The thorny paths of life he knew;
    His tender heart was quick to feel;
And wounds his pity wept to view,
    His bounty glowed to heal.
Of worldly ways, of frailty's slips,
    Of mortal sin, he had his share;
Yet still could breathe, with childhood's lips,
    His artless childhood's prayer.

IV.

Good deeds were all the work he wrought;
    Sweet thoughts and merry all he prized;
Nor power nor fame by him was sought,
    Nor humble things despised.
Strife could not live before his face,
    But, wheresoe'er his footsteps fell
Came kindness, with its smile of grace,
    And everything was well.

V.

He did not strive to win the heights:
  Enough for him the lowly vale,
The autumn sunset's pensive lights,
  The autumn's perfumed gale.
But toilers on the upward slope,
  Who greatly strove and bravely dared,
Had cheer of him, and felt new hope,
  Howe'er their fortune fared.

VI.

To brighten life, where'er he went,
  With laughter's sparkle, and to make
Home's fireside lovely with content,
  For gentle humour's sake —
This was his fate. Ah, darkly shows
  The path where yesterday he shone, —
That downward path of many woes
  That we must tread alone.

VII.

Yet he, like us, had lost and grieved:
  He knew how hard it is to bear,

When, lone and listless and bereaved,
   We sink in dumb despair.
And could those lips, now marble chill,
   But speak once more from that true heart,
With what a jocund, blithe good-will
   They 'd bid our grief depart!

VIII.

It was but yesterday he went:
   This is the room and that the door:
When some few idle days are spent
   'T will all be as before:
The heavenly morning will destroy
   This rueful dream of death and pain,
And I shall hear him say "My boy,"
   And clasp his hand again.

WHITE ROSES.

I.

MORE strange than death to all regrets,
   Love gives no tear to passion sped:
Its frozen heart at once forgets
   The wronged, the absent, and the dead.
We see the wave that Venus rides —
We do not see the doom it hides.

II.

Fierce, boundless, fetterless, supreme,
   Relentless, glorious, mindless, gay,
Love grants us one supernal dream,
   One vision, one ecstatic day;
In Fate's dull book one fiery page —
   Of bliss an hour, of woe an age.

III.

Be the red roses nevermore
   Companions to a thought of mine!
Behind me fades the lessening shore,
   Above, the stars of midnight shine;
On black and dangerous seas they gleam,
And life is done with doubt and dream.

IV.

Pale spectres of all dead desire,
   Ye wandering souls of heavenly light,
So lovely in your soft attire,
   So coldly pure, so sadly bright,
Henceforth be angels of my fate,
And take the life ye consecrate!

V.

White roses for the cradled head,
   The bridal veil, the stainless pall!
When love and sin and grief are dead,
   Let the white roses shroud them all!
Ah! bloom for me while time flows on,
And guard my rest when I am gone.

IN SANCTUARY.

I.

WHILE pale with rage the wild surf springs
    Athwart the harbor bar,
The safe ships fold their snowy wings,
    Beneath the evening star:
In this calm haven rocked to sleep,
    All night they swing and sway,
Till mantles o'er the morning deep
    The golden blush of day.

II.

Here, safe from every storm of fate,
    From worldly strife and scorn,
Thus let me fold my hands and wait
    The coming of the morn;
While all night long, o'er moon-lit turf,
    The wind brings in from far
The moaning of the baffled surf
    Athwart the harbor bar.

www.ingramcontent.com/pod-product-compliance
Lightning Source LLC
Chambersburg PA
CBHW032158160426
43197CB00008B/975